Japan
made easy

japan
made easy

sandeep goyal

HarperCollins *Publishers* India

First published in India by
HarperCollins *Publishers* in 2019
Building No 10, Tower A, 4th Floor, DLF Cyber City, Phase II,
Gurugram – 122002
www.harpercollins.co.in

1 2 3 4 5 6 7 8 9 10

P-ISBN: 978-93-5357-007-1
E-ISBN: 978-93-5357-008-8

Typeset in 12/15.3 Requiem at
Manipal Digital Systems, Manipal

Fumio Oshima
The One
who
guided me
advised me
influenced me
motivated me
inspired me
encouraged me
spurred me
galvanized me
applauded me
blessed me
through my Japan journey

Contents

II: AESTHETICS

III: CULTURE

IV: FOOD

V: PHILOSOPHY OR WAY OF LIFE

VI: SOCIAL

VII: SPIRITUAL

VIII: SPORTS AND RECREATION

FOREWORD

When Sandeep Goyal requested me to write the foreword to his book, *Japan Made Easy*, two thoughts came to my mind. The first was *Reiwa*, the new era that started on 1 May 2019. The second was the 2020 Olympics which Tokyo will host next year.

The *kanji* characters for *Reiwa* are derived from the Man'yōshō, an eighth-century (Nara period) anthology of *waka* poetry. The *kotobagaki* (headnote) to this compilation in verse, when translated into English, reads as follows:

> *It was in new spring, in a fair (rei) month,*
> *When the air was clear and the wind a gentle (wa) breeze.*
> *Plum flowers blossomed a beauty's charming white*
> *And the fragrance of the orchids was their sweet perfume.*

Reiwa is best interpreted as 'beautiful harmony'. This, in many ways is also the essence of Japan as a country. I am glad that Goyal's book dwells in detail on the beauty and harmony that essentially defines Japan, covering different dimensions of the same in its traditions, customs, culture, food, society, arts, business and more, through well-researched and insightful essays.

Japan will host the 2020 Olympics, with 'Discover Tomorrow' as the theme of the games, where the endeavour is to convey that the never-changing nature of Japanese culture is that it's always changing. The Olympics will showcase how the Japanese combine tradition with cutting-edge technology and innovation, while lavishing the famed *omotenashi* Japanese hospitality on guests. As a result, visitors from India and from the world over, will surely end up experiencing how Japan is so cool, and Tokyo is so much fun! Goyal's book is therefore very timely. It offers simple insights on Japan that will help potential visitors appreciate and understand the finer nuances of the experience that is in store for them.

Japan Made Easy clearly demonstrates the deep understanding that Goyal has of Japanese business too. The fact that he himself was a joint-venture partner of a large advertising agency from Japan, and has over the years worked closely with major global Japanese clients comes through very clearly in his nuanced explanations on how to, and how not to, approach business in Japan. The narratives, the examples and the explanations are simple but solid. A good and enriching read.

I wish Goyal and *Japan Made Easy* all the success, and hope readers will enjoy the 101 essays in the book that cover everything from *sushi* to *sake*, and *sama* to *sumo*.

Sanjay Kumar Verma, IFS
Indian Ambassador to Japan

INTRODUCTION

Japan Made Easy was born as a book in my mind perhaps twenty years ago. I used to visit Japan almost every month on work those days. And almost every evening, post work, we would end up at an *enkai,* more popularly referred to as a *nomikai* (drinking party) at an *izakaya* (bar-restaurant, more like a tavern) or a traditional *ryoutei-*style establishment somewhere not far from the office. The *ryoutei* would have a large *tatami* (a special mat on the floor of a traditional Japanese room) with small low tables or trays arranged in a large square or rectangular formation, depending on the head-count. Behind everyone there would be a small floor pillow to sit on. Each of us would take our places, sitting in the traditional *seiza* position which needs you to kneel and sit on the soles of your feet (and I, with my not so inconsiderable size, would find it most difficult to sit in that posture!). Almost everyone from our work group would be present; the jackets would be taken-off; the neck-ties loosened; the leader of the group would make a speech in Japanese (translated in bits and pieces into English by one of my Japanese colleagues for my benefit); and then the drinking would begin.

Etiquette at a *nomikai* demands that one doesn't pour one's own alcohol, be it beer, whisky, *sake*, or *shochu* (a strong Japanese hard liquor, quite like vodka). Instead, one is supposed to offer to fill the glasses of others for them. Traditionally, younger colleagues in the company pour for those higher up. This is especially true of *senpai-kōhai* (senior-junior) relationships, where the participant of lower rank or age will first offer to serve his superior. This relationship is often reciprocal, and the superior will offer to fill the junior's glass in return. This is not perceived so much as currying favour as it is seen as acting in a manner conducive to workplace harmony (referred to in Japanese society as *wa*). There would then be a lot of eating and drinking. Actually, more drinking than eating. And the Japanese would merrily mix their drinks, switching from beer to whisky to *sake* and *shochu* without following any particular order or applying any restraints, and chat, criticize and argue. There would be a lot of frank and emotional conversation. Stuff you would never broach at work. They call it *bureikō* in Japanese. Basically, letting your hair down.

But what would really fascinate me every time at the *nomikai* would be the traditional clapping at the *shime* (ending) of the party, when everyone would stand up and clap in unison. There are two styles of clapping : *ippon-jime* and *sanbon-jime*. The *ippon-jime* was the 'one-clap ending' while *sanbon-jime* was the three-clap version. The three-clap ending would be three series of three claps, followed by a single clap. This would be repeated three times, taking the total number of claps to thirty. All for teamwork, and greater success together.

But the party would not end there. Post the *nomikai*, some of my friends would lead me to a *nijikai* or after-party. And that would most times extend into *sanjikai* or bar-hopping thereafter.

The *nomikai* in many ways triggered *Japan Made Easy*. Here was this society, so opaque and insular to the world outside. So work-obsessed, so regimented and so mechanical when seen through Western eyes. But so very friendly, intimate and closely knit together when you got to know them up close. So much fun too. I thought Japan merits explanation, it needs someone to look at society there, the culture, the philosophy, the way they do business, actually for someone to look inside the head of a typical Japanese and interpret how he thinks, how he dreams, what he wants, what he fears. And more. And use that as a mirror to what anyone outside Japan would want to know about the country, its customs, its culture and its cumulative consciousness.

I chose to write and format *Japan Made Easy* a bit differently. Today, we are all so used to heading to Google's search engine for anything and everything that we want to know or research. Well, I decided to take 101 key words and phrases that I thought best represented a wholesome picture of Japan, and decode, demystify, and explain them. Be a Google to my readers. Adding of course local insights, local flavours, local nuances and local interpretations from my many years of knowing (and loving) Japan.

So that is what *Japan Made Easy* is all about. A closer look at Japan. A closer look at its aesthetics, business, culture, food, philosophy, society, spirituality, even entertainment and sport.

Japan is a country I love. In fact adore. I love its beauty, I love its people. I love it customs, I love its culture. I even love its idiosyncrasies.

Through *Japan Made Easy*, I hope to bring the Japan that I love to you. For you to savour, for you to soak in, for you to understand, for you to appreciate, for you to enjoy.

BUSINESS

1

AMAKUDARI

The term *amakudari*, literally translated, means 'descent from heaven'.

Amakudari is derived from Japanese mythology. Ancient tales from the country tell of how the gods descended from heaven to earth and became the ancestors of the Japanese emperor and his family. Today, *amakudari* denotes the unique Japanese institutional practice where elite bureaucrats retire to related government institutions and private companies, and continue to lord over them. The metaphor is intended to show how powerful the elite bureaucrats are in Japan. They are recognized as the new gods of the country's firmament, who rule when in employment, and continue to carry great influence and power even when they retire!

Amakudari is a self-perpetuating virtuous (or vicious) cycle of shared goodness and almost denotes state-sponsored generosity. It is the Japanese way of extending the tenure of bureaucrats beyond retirement age, and providing them powerful and lucrative sinecures. For the bureaucrat, an extended tenure in a new avatar is of course a reward for lifelong service, an appreciation and compensation for loyalty and commitment. For the government or corporate entities, it is an easy way of perpetuating patronage, and a well-planned methodology of retaining trusted hands in key positions.

Amakudari become effective ambassadors for their new employers, acting as trusted bridges to their old alma maters. In real terms, they are influential power brokers who push through decisions, even legislations, that favour their principals or clients because of their easy access to old colleagues and their ability to access inside information. As powerful lobbyists, *amakudari* help private firms reach levels of government that are otherwise not easy to influence. They are therefore of vital importance in shaping government policy towards industry, or towards a particular business house. What is even more important is that the institution of *amakudari* works with a certain self-confidence and sure-footed self-assurance that can only come from many years of traversing a familiar terrain.

Amakudari isn't limited to the bureaucracy – *amakudari*-like processes exist between large firms and small firms, amongst businesses within a *keiretsu* (business conglomerates), amongst banks, and even amongst educational institutions. So although it's important to understand and acknowledge *amakudari*'s existence, it's equally important to realize the magnitude and astonishing reach of this condescending practice which has, via collusion with other societal institutions, built itself up into an almost impregnable fortress.

The practice of *amakudari* is one that dates back to Imperial Japan. The system of rewarding retiring bureaucrats was prevalent even then. Only, perhaps, it was not as blatant. Or so in the face. In modern-day Japan, it is almost a scourge. Corruption personified. A consolation prize for the old war horse. Also, a second lease of life in the corridors of power. This time as a facilitator, rather than as a decision maker. Some bureaucrats become so adept at liaisoning that they actually wear many hats concurrently, which is termed as *urakudari* in Japan.

As an article titled 'Amakudari remains an issue' published by the *Japan Times* in 2017 said, *amakudari* has often drawn criticism for 'creating cosy, corrupt relations'. Initiatives to snuff out *amakudari* have been numerous, but have largely remained toothless and unsuccessful. Post the Second World War, *amakudari* has weathered the many slings and arrows directed at it; yet, it has persisted and prospered, and become even more entrenched and institutionalized.

2

CHUKAI-SHA

A *chukai-sha* is a 'go-between', a really precious resource in a society that is so very closed to outsiders. For those wanting to do business with Japan, the hiring of a *chukai-sha* can sometimes become the difference between success and failure. The *chukai-sha* opens doors, creates openings, helps negotiations, gathers feedback and takes business to places it may not have gone on its own.

Typically, the *chukai-sha* are retired seniors of large corporations. They enjoy stature which opens many doors and many opportunities. When doing business in Japan, having a well-placed 'go-between' saves you a lot of hassle and bother. It is not that the Western world is not familiar with liaison men, but the typical *chukai-sha* is a more evolved and polished being.

But before we even get to the *chukai-sha*, we need to understand two other related concepts: *shokaijo* and *jin-myaku*. The *shokaijo* is a formal introduction that forms the basis for the start of a business relationship in Japan. This introduction is valuable as it comes from a trusted source and can be relied upon. The *chukai-sha* is either himself well placed enough to initiate the *shokaijo*, or will have the necessary and relevant outreach to source someone credible enough to make the introduction. And an introduction well made is invariably a good door-opener. *Jin-myaku* refers to a personal network of contacts. Japanese businessmen are very wary of doing business with individuals or organizations they do not know. However, if someone comes with the reference of a person in their *jin-myaku*, it provides the desired assurance and legitimacy, hastening the start of a business partnership. It is again here that the *chukai-sha* play a pivotal role in smoothening the take-off.

Some *chukai-sha* become very powerful in the Japanese business system, becoming akin to power brokers in orchestrating deals. For outsiders with limited access to the inner workings of a Japanese corporation, the *chukai-sha* has the benefit of being the person with the maximum knowledge and understanding of what is actually happening. And such knowledge means a lot of power.

This brings us to another couple of interesting concepts, of the *insei* and *ogosho*. The *insei* was a historical concept where a retired emperor would continue to wield power, albeit behind the scenes. Old, retired *chukai-sha* are somewhat similar to the *insei*. Retired, but relevant. And powerful. With powerful connections and friends, they can immensely benefit a business. Similarly *ogosho*, originally the residence of retired *shoguns*, is in modern times more a reference to the top shots in any domain. A good *chukai-sha* would have connections with such *insei* and *ogosho*, ensuring a more beneficial progress of business.

Over time, *chukai-sha* have become more outgoing and more innovative. The better ones are investing in actually setting up the equivalent of liaison offices, staffed with English-speaking Japanese for a better understanding of clients, and better communications too. Some are bringing in research staff. Basically, the *chukai-sha* today are stretching themselves to serve their clients better, and are willing to invest in building relationships and rapport. Results, they know from experience, will follow.

3

DOUKI

ouki refers to colleagues who join a company at the same time. Batchmates, as they would be called in any other part of the world.

Japanese companies hire a reasonably large number of fresh college graduates every year, and then train them to fit into their corporate culture. Many of them remain in the same company until retirement. Colleagues who join a company in the same year are called *douki*.

The origin of the word *douki* can perhaps be traced back to a very famous military song from the Pacific War period that goes, 'You and I are the cherry blossoms of *douki*, so why don't we fall beautifully for the nation together,' which seems to indicate that the word *douki* meant something special for the soldiers way back then. The lifelong bond between *douki* is like that of professional brothers and there is a lot of value ascribed to the relationship. A *douki* is a cross between a sibling and a comrade – the unwritten agreement is that all *douki* will stick together, whatever happens. They work together, organize drinking parties together, invite each other to their weddings, keep in touch and communicate with each other for decades, often beyond retirement.

In the 'vertical society' of Japan, *douki* is a unique source of 'horizontal' friendship. *Douki* tend to help each other not only with their work, but also with their private lives. Examples abound of *douki* helping each other along in their careers just out of that one bond of professional brotherhood. Equally, they provide a comforting shoulder to each other when the work atmosphere at the *kaisha* (company) becomes too difficult or too demanding. After all, the relationship of *douki* is all about the shared memories of having cut their teeth together. A shared journey, shared joys, and shared highs and lows.

But, at the same time, it must be acknowledged that the *douki* relationship can fray over the years; in fact, it can sometimes become a source of rivalry. In the initial years, *douki* gatherings are mostly all about drinking and dining together, and having a good time, exchanging news and gossip about work and common acquaintances. At some point of time, however, some *douki* start to climb up the corporate ladder, while the rest get left behind. So, they remain friendly on the surface, but gradually the relationship becomes estranged in reality. But in Japan, this is really an exception to the rule as it is ingrained in the *douki* relationship that like brothers in a family, some are bound to prosper more and some less, but that is not to affect their mutual ties.

One must understand that *douki* friendships are far more deep-rooted than those of school or college classmates. They have parallels to the similar deep bonds between cadets in military schools. Much like the army, these *douki* would work together for the same organization for almost their entire working lives, staying together for maybe four decades in a lifelong employment. So, there is a certain permanency and longevity to the *douki* relationship, which goes beyond just spending a few years together in a school or college, and then going your own individual ways.

4

GARAPAGOSU SHOUKOUGUN

The phrase *garapagosu shoukougun* translates as 'Galapagos Syndrome'.

This is a buzzword which gained currency around 2007. It describes the Japanese tendency to develop products and services to overly fit their own tastes and rules, consequently failing to adapt to the rest of the global market. The term 'Galapagos Syndrome' or, 'Galapagos-ization', refers to the process of the isolation of the Japanese and their islandic 'Galapagos-thinking'. The term is used as an analogy to a part of Charles Darwin's *The Origin of Species*. Darwin came across in the Galapagos Islands secluded flora and fauna, which evolved differently from what he saw elsewhere. This phenomenon was a key to the advancement of his theory of evolution.

The particular phenomenon that helped the phrase *garapagosu shoukougun* gain momentum was the difficulty the Japanese cellphone industry was facing. Until the first half decade of the twenty-first century, Japanese cellphones were by far the leaders across the world in terms of ideas and technologies. In 1999, the Japanese firm NTT Docomo introduced its innovative 'i-mode' mobile series, which enabled cellphones to connect to the internet for the first time in history. At that time, this feature was at least five years ahead of the rest of the world. Moreover, Japanese cellphones kept adding unique features such as e-money, e-tickets and netbanking functions, cameras, TV monitors, and much more. This obviously stimulated a Steve Jobs to deliberate on the invention of the iPhone, which metamorphosed and redefined the mobile market worldwide. The problem therefore was that the Japanese cellphone industry, despite its early lead and advantage, was satisfied with merely prospering in the Japanese market, never really trying to reach out and conquer the markets overseas. Hence, *garapagosu shoukougun.*

In the meantime, the then Finnish Nokia and the Korean Samsung expanded their share in the global market with their simpler and cheaper models, taking for themselves the bottom-end of the market. And, in the end, the introduction of the smartphone devastated the whole concept and technology of the i-mode; entirely taking away from Japan what could have been a world-beater opportunity.

The problem with Japan is that many pioneering ideas, like for example, the Suica, the rechargeable contactless smart card, which like electronic money was used as a fare card on train lines in the country, are way way ahead of their times. But Japanese companies failed to export and monetize the idea and technologies to other parts of the world. The isolationism of Japan can well be understood from the fact that across the country, many ATMs might not accept bank and credit cards that have been issued outside of the country!

Garapagosu shoukougun is now used in Japan not only to describe the marketing failure of products and services, but the general mentality that brings about such a failure as well. In many ways, perhaps the homogeneous culture of the Japanese people has potentially created the danger of narcissistic evolution. At the same time, may be Galapagos-ness is one of Japan's great charming points: if the entire world would be the same, then what would be unique or different?

5

GOTOUBI

❧

otoubi is the term used in Japan to refer to dates that are in multiples of five in every month: five, ten, fifteen, twenty, twenty-five, and thirty. These are, apparently, the busiest days for business in Japan, and in folklore are ordained as such by accountants.

Gotoubi perhaps dates back to a practice in the golden Edo period, when businesses used to close their accounts in five-day cycles. There was an old custom of selling goods on the basis of five-day *yakusoku tegata,* or 'promissory notes' – Japan's earliest form of credit notes. *Gotoubi* continued well into the 1980s, tapering off somewhat in later years. With that also died the institution of *soroban,* or 'abacuses', small print shops that produced ready-made billing forms, and a legion of bill collectors.

In fact, it used to be said that post the Second World War on *gotoubi* days, traffic would peak in Tokyo as all businesses were out on the road, squaring up the books by personally visiting clients.

Some say the practice of *gotoubi* was derived from the Japanese system of keeping business credit in control. Credit was extended through promissory notes that would expire in five days, resulting in the dates of five of every month becoming settlement days. This ensured the safety of funds for the business, and also ensured liquidity. It also became a reason to visit clients and increase one-to-one interaction, resulting in enhanced business and better service.

The practice of *gotoubi* may have waned over the years with larger Japanese companies switching to just two main days, the twenty-fifth and the thirtieth of every month, as settlement days or pay-out days. But financial markets even now, especially those dealing with forex, do report upward blips on *gotoubi* days. Data on this is not unequivocal, but forex managers insist it happens. They maintain that there is always a real and enhanced demand for the US dollar on *gotoubi* days, and any downside on the dollar is normally limited to these 'multiples-of-five' days.

With regard to the traffic snarls, it is easy to get caught in one in Tokyo or Osaka, and to be cheerfully told by your Japanese colleague that it usually happens on *gotoubi* days. True or false, Tokyo (and Osaka) are always crowded, and *gotoubi* or not, traffic snarls are a part of everyday Japan. So to attribute the traffic rush to the time-old five-day settlement is now largely notional and conversational, and not as real as it used to be.

But one thing is for sure: if you are doing business with Japan, or visiting Japan on business, it would be prudent to avoid the *gotoubi* dates of the twenty-fifth and the thirtieth of the month because everyone is so very busy with payments, collections, audit and stock taking. So these are two days of the calendar month to not ask for or expect to get appointments with your Japanese counterparts. The *gotoubi* may have weakened over the years, but it still works in practice, howsoever limited.

6

HANKO

❧

If there is a visible symbol of Japanese bureaucracy, it is the traditional *hanko*, the name-stamp or name-seal. The *hanko* has also been referred to as the 'chops', though whether this description is driven by its annihilatory powers or is just a name that has become popular over time is something one cannot be sure about.

The *hanko* name-stamp is used by the Japanese in lieu of actually signing a document or contract. This is especially true of documents that are formal or official in nature. The important thing is that a document of significance may require a dozen, or sometimes even more, *hankos*. What is interesting is that most of this *hanko* stamping follows a well-defined and time-tested sequence. In effect, if one of the worthies who is to approve the document and affix his *hanko*, is on vacation, or otherwise preoccupied, then the document can indefinitely go on hold. What is even more scary is the possibility that one of the officers in the *hanko* chain may not agree with the contents of the document and may either decide to not cooperate or just abstain from stamping it, bringing the approval process to a screeching standstill. The worst fate of course that can befall a document is internal politics within the organization, and possible dissent. An officer may decide to belittle the originator of the document (and the project) because of an internal disagreement, or may have a point of view that has previously not been addressed, and this may result in one or more of the officers desisting from putting his *hanko* on the document, leading to a go-slow. Or even a slow death.

The torturous journey of official documents through the many *hanko* starts and stops is the stuff that scares a lot of Westerners doing business with Japan. If negotiating, say, a joint venture in Tokyo, when everything has been largely agreed upon, the final signing, or more appropriately, the *hanko* stamping of the shareholders agreement may be all that is left. The tension of the *hanko* process can even lead the most hard-boiled foreign businessmen into a depression. It is not just the time that the process consumes but its capacity that stumps outsiders. The *hanko* is a symbol of power, and so it is exercised. Of course, none of it is crass or in the face. It is just a process followed as a matter of fact, and obstructed equally as a matter of fact!

One of the biggest matters of pride therefore for a foreigner doing business in Japan is to be gifted a personalized *hanko*. To have a name-stamp surely gives one a feeling of vicarious power! Not that you will ever end up stamping too many important documents, but it is nevertheless a possession that can proudly be displayed on your work desk. You, of course, also need to know that your *hanko* needs to be officially registered (*natsuin*) to make it a valid official name-seal.

The *hanko* persists in Japan despite the signature being the norm in most global societies now. It is a visible stamp of authority, and so it will stay for at least some time to come.

7

HATARAKIKATA KAIKAKU

Hatarakikata Kaikaku is to 'reform the way we work'.

Long working hours have been the norm in Japan for as long as one can remember. Despite repeated acts of *karoshi,* or 'dying from overwork', there has been no improvement in the harsh working conditions in Japanese companies. In 2017, in fact, the ministry of health, labour and welfare released its first ever white paper on *karoshi* (death from overwork). The fact that the ministry had to publish such a paper is a chilling reminder of the cruelty of the country's workplace environment.

But a twenty-four-year-old female employee's suicide from overwork at a top ad agency in 2015 tipped the balance at last. Ever since, *Hatarakikata Kaikaku,* or 'reforming the way we work', has become the buzzword in Japanese business circles. The government is actively looking to change work environments. In fact, Prime Minister Shinzo Abe has placed himself at the head of a panel dedicated to this goal, wanting 'to turn Japan into a country that rejects the workaholic mentality'.

During Japan's high-growth years, long hours at work were rewarded and appreciated. The more people worked, the more affluent they became. But now, the Japanese need to work long hours to ensure that they do not lose their jobs. On top of all this is the disheartening news that Japan's productivity statistics show that they are lagging behind other advanced countries. That means, long hours are not necessarily bringing in better results, which many believe calls for more work. It is a vicious cycle.

Prime Minister Abe has appointed a designated minister to handle this onerous reform work. Businesses are starting to crack down on overtime by forcing employees to leave earlier, turning off the lights at a certain time. But the real challenge is to promote productivity and achieve better results with less work. Otherwise, businesses would have to slow down.

Businesses are making efforts beyond forcing employees to leave early:

1. Giving incentives to those who come in early instead of leaving late for extra work.
2. Giving more flexible work-style choices such as tele-working and flexi time.
3. Instituting a rule to ask for permission before doing overtime.
4. Letting employees leave office at 3 pm on Fridays.
5. Being more liberal with 'care' leaves. Basically encouraging employees to be more involved with family.
6. Encouraging employees to utilize their paid holidays and not just let them accumulate or lapse.

But the problem is far more deep-rooted. All of these external actions mean little when the employees themselves, so used to long working hours, do not know what to do with this new enforced extra leisure time!

So, the ones who are so used to working hard all the time cannot just be weaned away or curtailed from working long hours. There are the employees who continue to work long hours, but do the extra hours off the record and do not let anyone know. There are others, taking advantage of the loosening company rules, who have started to look at plural employment. But work they must.

8

HESO WO MAGERU

Heso wo mageru colloquially translates to 'bending the belly button'. *Heso* is the belly button. And tinkering with it, or bending it, creates irritation which tantamounts to hurting someone's sentiments. Literally though, *Heso wo mogeru* means that someone's navel is off-centre. This expression has come to refer to someone who is difficult, uncooperative, and unreasonable.

The navel and the navel whorl of hair are normally centrally located. A person who is odd, perverse, intractable or cantankerous is described as *heso-magari* (out-of-line navel) or *tsumuji-magari* (off-centre whorl). *Heso wo mageru* (an off-centre navel) and *tsumuji wo mageru* (make the whorl off-centre) are the verb forms, meaning to get angry, act perverse or be spiteful without a justifiable cause. Although a person who 'puts his navel out of line' may not have a justifiable cause for doing so, in many cases he has an underlying reason – such as being left out of a thing or having been made to lose face. A *heso-magari* is usually a petty person, who is not 'manly'. Subordinates have to be careful not to push their boss into a position where his navel moves off-centre because then they will be the ones to suffer.

But the genesis of this phrase is rooted in the important understanding of a very Japanese concept: the stomach is seen as the centre of the body; unlike in the West, where the heart is considered the epicentre.

If in the Western world we say 'deep down from my heart', in Japan it would be phrased more like 'deep down from my stomach'.

When working with the Japanese, one needs to be very sensitive in handling day-to-day interactions. Sometimes, a very small slip or an unintended offence can leave one's Japanese counterpart very unhappy. The important thing is to understand that the negative stimuli can leave the Japanese with his stomach tied up in knots, and a poked belly button that can be very irritating. The problem also is that the Japanese never openly express disagreement or dissent. They just simmer, that too not externally or visibly. Their stomach hurts, but they will not let it be known. In fact, they will let the stomach churn with the hurt, but will maintain a stoic silence in front of everyone. In reality, this can be very dangerous, because, a Japanese spurned is a Japanese best avoided!

To spot a bent *heso* requires sensitizing oneself to non-verbal and subtle signals from Japanese colleagues and counterparts who may feel annoyed or hurt. If you are smart, you also learn quickly enough that the *heso* can be righted through a round of drinks in the evening, and a sincere heart-to-heart (no, stomach-to-stomach!) chat.

Recognizing *heso wo mageru*, however, is not easy for a non-Japanese. Many a times, the slight may actually be unintentional or unintended. But the Japanese belly button is really sensitive. It hurts, and it hurts hard. A reprimand in public view. A raised voice. A rebuke in a mail also copied to juniors. The *heso* is really vulnerable.

Back to the Japanese stomach versus the Western heart. Much as, for most of us, the heart bleeds, in Japan the stomach revolts, making the *heso* the trigger of disaffection. Avoid!

9

HIKANZEI SHOUHEKI

Hikanzei Shouheki are nothing but 'non-tariff barriers'.
To global competitors, the Japanese market remains more opaque than most others because of deep cultural differences – the way Japanese society is structured portrays, in many ways, its economy to the outside world.

Japan's complex distribution system, its emphasis on long-term relationships and procedures that depend more on discretion than on law – all of these can confound foreign business executives who fail to understand the island nation's culture. The Japanese market is difficult to break into even for local players, and until recently, their bankruptcy rate was six times that of the United States.

Despite the generally perceived notions, the Japanese market is rather open to imports in terms of tariff. In Japan, there has been no tariff on automobiles since 1978, while the US still maintains 2.5 per cent tariff and EU 10 per cent. Even the tariff for agricultural produce in Japan, which is believed to be very high, remains lower than in the countries of the EU.

Then where does Japan's image of a 'closed market' come from? Perhaps from non-tariff barriers. In other words, local regulations, business systems, customs and cultures. Three kinds of trade barriers can be easily assessed and compared: tariffs, quotas and visible non-tariff barriers, such as voluntary export restraints. In each of these Japan compares favourably with other countries.

It is not as much the visible barriers as the invisible ones that arouse American anger. It is complaints about the Japanese insistence on inspecting American factories and sometimes even individual products before admitting goods into Japan. Japan may invariably not accept testing data from labs in the United States, so products must be subjected to the delay and expense of further testing. That is what frustrates foreign companies.

There is the famous case of the baseball bats from the 1980s that is very often quoted as an example of Japanese obstructionism. For many years, the United States kept putting pressure on Japan to permit imports of America-made aluminium baseball bats. In 1982, Japan relented and modified seventeen laws and safety standards. Even then, only one company, after energetically pursuing the Japanese market, sold only 250 bats in a full year!

But then there is also the story of McDonald's in Japan. The legendary Den Fujita saw an opportunity the Americans themselves did not see. Fujita launched McDonald's in Japan in 1971 in the belief that the reason Japanese people are generally short is because they have eaten nothing but fish and rice for two thousand years. 'If we eat McDonald's hamburgers and potatoes for a thousand years, we will become taller, our skin will become white, and our hair blonde,' he said, as mentioned in the book, *Fast Food Nation: The Dark Side of the All-American Meal* (Mariner Books, 2013). McDonald's today has 3,800 restaurants in Japan. Fujita succeeded with an

American product and an American brand. Not only McDonald's but Disney too has been a massive success in Japan. Which only goes to prove that if done right, Japan is as easy or as difficult as any other global market to win or lose.

10

IHYO WO TSUKU

*I*hyo wo tsuku means 'to surprise'. It is one of the favourite negotiating strategies of the Japanese: springing a surprise.

Surprises of the *ihyo wo tsuku* type are intended to catch the other side off guard, giving the Japanese team a negotiating edge. The surprises can vary. A sudden declaration of withdrawal from the negotiations, without notice or reason. Tabling a completely new proposal when the earlier discussions were almost near closure or agreement. Introducing a new team to the negotiating table. Accusing the other side of insincerity. Completely changing the technology transfer construct; all ploys designed to completely throw the other side in disarray and dismay!

The Japanese are normally very formal, very agenda driven and very polite in any negotiation. This tends to perhaps lower the guard of the other party, especially foreigners. It is in such a situation that a clever Japanese negotiator trumps the opposing side with surprise, a well-rehearsed and sharp business tactic, especially if the Japanese side is in a stronger bargaining position. Why do the Japanese do this? The Japanese are traditionally known to respond very slowly to changes or new developments in any business situation. *Ihyo wo tsuku* uses this very Japanese weakness to advantage: because response to change is expectedly slow; why not derive benefit or profit by using a changed agenda in a negotiation to drive the other party into panic and unplanned chaos?

I have seen many more interesting *ihyo* strategies: the easiest being to change the specs of a project, citing 'internal' requirements. Another easy one is to vaguely refer to J-Sox compliance, without any specifics. The best one, of course, is to just keep introducing newer and newer members to the negotiating team and requesting for the presentation document to be altered to include a slightly different point of view every time, in consideration of the new member's domain. This can, over time and over half-a-dozen iterations, end up materially changing the negotiation goalpost.

The overarching intent of unleashing *ihyo wo tsuku* is to extract a major concession that had earlier not been included in the discussion. Since the negotiation is nearing the finish line, the other side has no choice but to either concede to the demand, or risk many months of negotiations coming to a naught. If the two parties involved in the negotiation are both Japanese, *ihyo wo tsuku* perhaps does not come as much of a surprise. Of course, the standard and practised response of the 'surprised' other side is one of shock and dismay, with loud protestations on how they would be ruined if the negotiations were not to proceed to immediate closure. Japanese associates will tell you how the weaker group of negotiators cringe and cry and beg the other side not to 'kill them'. The practised routine continues till some concessions are made by both parties enabling the resumption of the negotiation!

For foreigners, *ihyo wo tsuku* is best handled by tabling reciprocity in the negotiation. When the Japanese team asks for a major change, skilled foreigners often ask for a give and take so that the process remains an ongoing negotiation where they too are able to extract a reasonable pound of flesh. And the 'surprise' is somewhat diluted.

11

KANBAN

❦

Kanban is Japanese for 'visual signal' or 'card'.

It became the trigger for a Japanese manufacturing system in which the supply of components is regulated through the use of an instruction card sent down, and through the production line. It is said that in the late 1940s, Toyota found a better engineering process from a highly unlikely source: the supermarket. They noticed that store clerks restocked a grocery item based on their store's inventory, and not their vendor's supply imperatives. Only when an item was nearing sellout did the clerks order for more. The grocers' 'just-in-time' delivery process prompted Toyota engineers to rethink their methods and innovate a never-before approach – a *kanban* system – that would match inventory with demand, and achieve higher levels of not just quality but output too.

By better communication through visual management, Toyota line workers used a *kanban* (that is, an actual card) to signal steps in their manufacturing process. The system's highly visual approach allowed teams to communicate far more easily on what needed to be done, and when. It therefore standardized the signals and refined the processes, which helped reduce waste and maximize value.

Kanban in many ways helps you harness the power of visual information , such as using sticky notes on a whiteboard to create a 'picture' of your work. Showing the work flow within a team not only provides a status update but also showcases in detail how the progress is being made. *Kanban* takes information that would normally be communicated through words and turns it into brain candy.

Within Toyota, the credit for *kanban* is given to an industrial engineer, Taiichi Ohno. *Kanban* has over the years become an effective tool to support the running of a production system as a whole, and is an excellent way to promote improvement. Problem areas are highlighted by reduction in the number of *kanban* in circulation. One of the main plusses of *kanban* is to set an upper limit to the work-in-process inventory, and therefore prevent the overloading of the manufacturing system.

An English-language term that closely captures the meaning of *kanban* is 'queue limiter', and the beneficial result is 'queue limitation'. Operationally, these process problems are then dealt with. The 'queue limit' (or the maximum limit allowed) needs to be reduced; for example, a former upper limit of five pieces is reduced to four, with 'queue time' in the process reduced by 20 per cent.

Kanban is today a universal concept adopted by industries far beyond the originators, Toyota. The *kanban* thought, and process, is used by many Western companies both in manufacture and in transport, bringing efficiency to their operations. Today, management consultants have found myriad applications for *kanban* across industries, including e-commerce and digital businesses.

If one is not from a manufacturing background, one may not be able to fully understand *kanban* or internalize its benefits. But were one to ever sit with a Japanese team and watch them work, one would be fascinated by how many of them have Post-it notes of different colours pasted on their clipboards and how they keep scribbling new reminders on them. This may not be *kanban*, but it surely signals a more methodical and orderly way of working.

12

KANDAN

The Japanese word *kandan* can be interpreted in English as 'pleasant talk or chat' or 'quiet conversation' or 'idle talk'. *Kandan* can also be referred to as an informal meeting. Especially an after-hours meeting.

Kandan plays an important role in the conduct of business in Japan. As an outsider, more so as a foreigner, it could take you a while to figure out that what transpired outside office is equally, if not more, important than what took place in office. Much of the work and the meetings follow a predictable pattern. But once you are done with 'work', the actual work actually begins. The office spills over to a nice restaurant or a restobar, and then over many rounds of beer, *sake, shochu* and whisky, and endless rounds of good food, your Japanese colleagues open up.

While this informal interaction is a good diversion after a long day's work, you soon realize that there is hardly a dividing line between what is official and what is casually discussed in the evening. If you happen to work with a Japanese company, or do extensive business with them, especially if you visit Japan quite often, *kandan* can be used beneficially to soften up officials on the other side. The only problem, piquant as it does sometimes prove to be, is that the seriousness of formal meetings wanes in the face of too much *kandan*.

Sometimes getting the Japanese to visit you at your home when they visit your country can also be quite useful. The proverbial Japanese 'pleasant talk' or *kandan* can be used to soften intimidating reputations in the cosy confines of a private living room, where it is much easier for everyone to relax and open up.

The only problem with *kandan* is that all conversations with the Japanese are in their own language and that makes it very uncomfortable for outsiders who neither understand what is being discussed nor can participate in the conversation. The only noticeable exception is when one meets a Japanese person from an overseas division of a company. Most such Japanese persons speak good English (most likely have been educated in the US), and the conversation can be in a language both can speak and understand. In a mixed group, there is always an effort by the Japanese to have someone constantly translate key words and key components of the conversation to the visitor, but this is inefficient and ineffective.

Kandan is ideally suited to resolving acrimonious matters. In most parts of the world, board meetings are the forum for discussion and debate on all kinds of issues confronting the company. In Japan, most difficult matters are resolved through *nemawashi*, or consensus, in behind-the-scene confabulations, and the offsite evenings are a good venue for dispute redressal. By the time a matter is brought before the board, there is near unanimity on the agenda between the directors – the convergence having been hammered in by their deputies in many, many meetings in the office and outside. Especially using the easy familiarity of *kandan*.

13

KANGAETE OKIMASU

Kangaete okimasu literally means 'I will think about it'.

But before we discuss *kangaete okimasu*, it is important to understand the concept of *ishin denshin*, or tacit communication, in which both sides know what the other means without being direct. As said before, *kangaete okimasu* literally means 'I will think about it', but once you get to know the Japanese, you learn that it actually is a polite euphemism for a 'no'. But the Japanese will never say that to your face. It is the polite, evasive, mild-mannered *kangaete okimasu* which still holds out hope and still sounds more like a 'maybe' rather than an outright 'no'.

But things are beginning to change. Not only with foreigners, but the Japanese are starting to speak more assertively to other Japanese as well. The newer generation still ponders over excuses to make before saying no, but doesn't really seem to need the crutch any more. But some say this is more a product of bad manners than of increased self-confidence in the younger lot. Even women, almost fully conditioned to always saying 'yes', are beginning to increasingly use the more limiting, 'yes, but ...', which is directionally closer to a 'no'.

For those doing business in Japan, the nuance of the phrase used in interaction can be very important. While *kangaete okimasu* could stop you in your tracks because of the intended 'no' which has been politely veiled, one can come across very similar phrases of varying nuances in the negations. *Kekko desu* literally means 'I am fine', but is actually closer to 'I would love some more, please ask me again'. On the other hand, *muzukashii desu ne* translates to 'It is difficult to do that', but in real life it actually is a statement for 'It is impossible to do'. Period. After one is told that it is pointless to pursue the matter. Sometimes, the answer proffered could be *Doryoku shimasu*, which means a more helpful and hopeful 'I will try', but really means 'Forget it'. Similarly, one could be led off-track by *Zensho shimasu*, which simply means 'I will take a proper step'. but someone who knows the underlying meaning knows it to be 'I won't have anything to do with that any more'.

The various shades of saying 'no' only illustrate and underline how difficult it is to do business in Japan. Politeness and courtesy can actually be misguiding. Those used to a direct communication culture find this very difficult to handle. Ambiguity in business communication is something to carefully watch out for. It is not that any miscommunication is intended, but the indirectness in declining something politely rather than a simple but direct 'no' reflects Japanese traditional contexts that value hierarchy, social harmony, and interpersonal relationships.

There is a famous story of former Japanese Prime Minister Eisaku Sato, who said '*Zensho shimasu*' to the former American President Richard Nixon. The Americans took it to be a 'yes' as they interpreted it as 'I will take a favourable action'. But those who understood what Sato san meant knew it was just the opposite! Months later, Nixon finally figured out the import of the Japanese leader's words. And he was furious!

14

KUURU BIZU

Kuuru Bizu or 'Cool Biz' is a government initiative targeted at energy conservation by reducing air conditioning in offices and public places.

The ministry of environment initiated Cool Biz in June 2005. Reflecting its mandates, all central government offices started to run office air conditioning temperatures at 28°C (82°F) until September. The ministry realized these temperatures meant 'Warm Biz' for employees as offices were earlier cooled to about 16°C (60°F) and the sudden increase in temperature meant that wearing a suit to office was unbearable. So a new dress code was recommended for the success of the green initiative. Government employees could now shed their jackets, long-sleeved shirts, and ties (hitherto unheard of in Japan's formal business culture). As per the Cool Biz dress code, short-sleeved shirts, cotton trousers and skirts were permitted.

The Japanese private sector did not take to Cool Biz at first. The overall reluctance to participate had perhaps less to do with the high-Fahrenheit temperatures inside offices, and more to do with summer dress codes. The Japanese business culture has always placed a high premium on conduct, appearance and respect. In this context, wearing anything deemed as casual attire to a meeting could cause real damage to a professional relationship.

In an effort to encourage corporate Japan to embrace Cool Biz, then Prime Minister Junichiro Koizumi became an early role model for the initiative. He made frequent public appearances without a jacket or tie. He even donned a short-sleeved shirt! This turned out to be great publicity for the programme. It provided the private sector with both the confidence and the encouragement required to allow the Cool Biz dress code to become the norm.

Apparel makers were quick to respond. As a matter of fact, it was Gunze, one of the leading apparel makers in Japan, who seized the opportunity and came up with the word *Kuuru Bizu*, or 'Cool Biz', corresponding to the government's request. In the summer of 2005, all department stores, shopping malls and garment shops were filled with new lines of Cool Biz business attires.

In the summer that followed the Great East Japan Earthquake in 2011, saving energy was no longer just an environmentally friendly initiative but a necessity. The government announced publicly that there were chances of energy shortages that summer. As a reasonable consequence, everybody cut down their use of air conditioners and the Cool Biz fashion spread as never before. Even the newscasters of major TV networks started wearing Cool Biz on air. This sort of success could only happen in a country like Japan, where national and individual goals always seem to coalesce.

Now, dress codes have been left to each company to decide on their own. So how loose and how far you can go depends on where you work. No jacket, no tie, short sleeves are allowed as a common understanding, but whether jeans are okay or what kind of shoes you can wear, or how colourful you can go, are different from company to company. The same goes with when to start and when to finish the Cool Biz style. Mostly, it starts in June and ends in September.

Due to the country's humid climate, traditional Japanese summer attires were always made loosely in order to let air inside. So in a way, it can be said that Japan just went back to its original concepts of traditional summer wear through *kuuru bizu*.

15

MADOGIWAZOKU

Literally, *madogiwa* means 'alongside the window' and as an extension of the same, *madogiwazoku* means 'the window tribe'.

Actually, *madogiwazoku* stands for someone who has been sidelined in a company. It is also refers to someone who is no longer useful to the organization, or is nearing the end of his career.

To understand the origin of this word, one has to appreciate that by their very nature, and cultural upbringing, the Japanese like to be busy at work, and eagerly accept positions of responsibility. However, sometimes employees who have passed their prime (or proven themselves unreliable) are given decreased workloads by their organizations. These workers are usually given a seat by the window, where they idle their workdays away. Hence, the phrase 'the window tribe'.

Most *madogiwazoku* employees are middle managers who have managerial titles (like *Bucho* or *Jicho*), but they have no subordinates and little responsibility. Japanese companies are traditionally hesitant to shed redundant staff, so the fate of the *madogiwazoku* is like that of in-house retirement.

From one perspective, this might not seem like a bad bargain for the window-seat employees. They continue to draw paychecks, but don't have to work much in return. However, few Japanese aspire to become *madogiwazoku*. Most people look upon such workers with a mixture of disdain and pity.

In group-oriented Japan, one's personal identity is closely tied to one's identity at work. Therefore, a worker who has been put out to pasture this way suffers from a loss of self-esteem, not to mention boredom.

There are some very important perspectives, however, to be learnt in dealing with 'the window tribe'.

First and foremost, *madogiwazoku* employees are starved for recognition and social company. A kind word from you, or an invite to a drink in the evening, and you can have a friend for life. While they may not publicly portray it, most of these sidelined souls are very bitter and critical of the system they are yoked to (and consider themselves a victim of). Hence, they are an easy and rich source of internal gossip, and many times have all the critical company news.

Rarely, but it is not impossible, *madogiwazoku* managers can bounce back into the system. Especially those who got moved to the window due to internal politics. In Japanese companies, dispensations do change and sometimes lucky ones can stage a comeback into the mainstream. One such example quickly comes to mind. The gentleman under reference used to be a relatively quiet team member at one of the companies. Then, slowly but surely, he got sidelined to the window. But some of his old business associates continued to remain in touch with him, and made it a point to carry him a gift every time they were in Japan. He was eternally grateful to be recognized and befriended. And then, lo and behold, he was touched one day by the magic wand of *douki*. A former batchmate rose to become the company's *kaicho* (chairman). The *madogiwazoku* gentleman was a great friend of the new *kaicho*. In no time, he said goodbye to the window he had long gazed out from and was suddenly 'powerful' again!

16

NANIWABUSHI: KIKKAKE/ SEME/UREI

For generations and generations, and for years and years, the Japanese have lived neatly choreographed lives with much etiquette and ceremony built into their daily routines and work. Everything in Japan is 'prescribed', and even day to day acts are to be performed as per defined social and cultural codes that have remained constant. One such interesting practice is the *naniwabushi* negotiation strategy that is both in keeping with the Japanese style of 'role playing', and yet out of character with the passive and orderly conduct of business in Japan.

The *naniwabushi* is an 'extreme' style of negotiation that dates back to the Edo period (1600–1868). It is patterned after the three-part ballads performed to tell the tales of chivalrous robbers, and the rise and fall of great families, etc., accompanied by *shamisen*, or the Japanese lute. The three phases of *naniwabushi* are:

the opening *kikkake* with the general background of the story, the narrative of the critical events, *seme*, and finally the *urei*, expressing pathos and sorrow at what has happened. *Naniwabushi* is all about emotion. It starts where logic ends. The dramatic abilities of the invoker of *naniwabushi* are, of course, critical for the success of the performance.

Naniwabushi in businesses goes something like this. Suppose you wish to negotiate revised payment terms for your contract due to the prevailing difficult business climate. You would first approach your lender or customer by giving a *kikkake*. The *kikkake* would be like a backgrounder about how good a partner you have been through the thick and thin of things, talk about what a good relationship your two organizations have enjoyed over the years and how the personal relationships go back many years, and so on. The next stage is to move to *seme* and talk about the disastrous effects of the recession on your business, how you have been cutting costs, how you are making your ends meet with great difficulty. But despite all the cost control, you will be able to survive only if some leniency is given to your payment terms. In the *urei*, you will need to explain what will happen if the request is not granted: you and your family will be on the streets. You can make it as melodramatic as possible. Pleading is not just okay, but actually mandatory!

Naniwabushi is artful, premeditated and calculated. And in Japan, it works. The more tragic and melodramatic it is, the easier it is for the Japanese listener to forget earlier contracts and commitments. Business people who do not show compassion in such circumstances will be condemned as being cold-hearted or mercenary. So, the script is almost pre-decided. It just has to be narrated well, acted with sincerity, and performed with a good deal of passion. *Kikkake, seme* and *urei* work really well in this somewhat unusual but effective dispute redressal mechanism.

Naniwabushi negotiations can be eye-openers. For a non-Japanese, they can be fascinating. Not all negotiations are as smooth or as pleasant as the one described above, but almost invariably, some positive outcomes do result from them.

17

NEMAWASHI

❧

Nemawashi has no real English translation. The closest equivalent perhaps is 'consensus'. The literal translation, though, is 'preparation before transplanting a tree'. *Ne* means roots; *mawasu* means go around. Or, to go around the roots to prepare for transplantation.

But the actual business meaning of *nemawashi* is to do behind-the-scenes groundwork in advance for any business meeting to build consensus and unanimity. *Nemawashi* is an informal process of quietly laying down the foundation for any discussion on a project; talking to all concerned people, even those at the bottom of the hierarchical pyramid (watering the roots), gathering support and feedback, and trying to build everyone's buy-in.

Over time, *nemawashi* has become a global business buzzword, more so since the 1980s. You cannot pursue any serious business endeavour in Japan without truly understanding the meaning and implications of the important concept of *nemawashi*. There are several phrases in English that have meanings similar to *nemawashi*, such as 'building consensus', 'getting people on the same page', 'getting buy-in', 'sending up a trial balloon', 'testing the waters', 'getting everyone to board the bandwagon', 'greasing the skids', 'behind-the-scenes persuasion', and even 'lobbying'. However, each of these terms has its own implications, and none of them fully captures the nuances of *nemawashi*. It being an ongoing organizational process rather than a one-time event.

In Japan, high-ranking people expect to be properly briefed on any new proposals, well before an official meeting. If they find out about something for the first time during the meeting, they will feel like they have not been shown due respect and their views have not been given due consideration, and they may reject the proposal for that reason alone. Thus, it's important to approach these seniors individually before the meeting and discuss every aspect of it with them. This provides an opportunity to table the proposal, and gauge their initial reaction. This is also a good chance to hear their inputs and include them in the proposal. This process is *nemawashi*.

In Japan, without adequate *nemawashi*, you cannot expect your proposal to be approved in any meeting. On the other hand, once proper *nemawashi* has been done, the proposal is only rarely rejected. If the proposal has to get rejected, it will get rejected in the behind-the-scenes *nemawashi*. This also ensures that there is no loss of face at the actual meeting, as the proposal would then never be tabled till unanimity and consensus have been achieved at all levels, and there is broad support for the proposal across the board. If perchance a proposal does reach a decision-making meeting without proper *nemawashi* in advance, one of the meeting members only has to get up and say, '*Kiitenai*', or 'I haven't heard about it in advance', and automatically the decision gets postponed.

Even in the Japanese Diet meetings, all the Diet members read their questions and answers from the paper in their hands, for which bureaucrats and party staff have prepared. The papers have gone through behind-the-scene *nemawashi* well in advance. It is only in rare cases, that Diet members question or make a statement out of the blue. When this happens, the Japanese media tends to treat it as a very shocking incident!

18

NENKO JORETSU

Nenko joretsu is a 'seniority-wage system' in Japan, built around promoting an employee in order of his or her proximity to retirement.

In Japan, lifelong employment has been the norm. Once hired by a large corporation, most employees, largely university graduates, retire from the same employer, going up the hierarchy in what is commonly referred to as *nenko joretsu*. This seniority system combines years of service with a well-calibrated system of rank and stature. Pay, perks, promotions and even hierarchical perceptions are governed by a never-failing *nenko joretsu* that is firmly entrenched and rigorously followed.

While in the West, young management graduates become assistant vice presidents or associate vice presidents in just a couple of years post their MBAs, in Japan new recruits stay in 'junior' positions for many years. In the Japanese ad agency business, for example, it is quite common to see management graduates take up to twenty years sometimes to earn the title of *bucho* (senior manager). This elevation would get them to the bottom of middle management at most, so to say. In the interim, however, they would have spent many stints of two to three years, or more, in different divisions, different cities, different job assignments, with different clients, and sometimes even in different countries. Hence, entry into management is hard-earned, and mostly well deserved.

Consequently, in Japan, under *nenko joretsu*, climbing up the seniority ladder is almost a matter of right because of years of loyalty to the company. A manager does not necessarily have to be an outstanding performer at an individual level. He needs to be a good manager of the team. Keeping the team focused on assigned tasks, maintaining interpersonal harmony and, most importantly, taking the blame when things go wrong, is the real making of a 'good' manager in Japan.

A shortcoming of *nenko joretsu* is that only permanent regular workers (*honko*) can receive the full benefit of *nenko joretsu*; other classes of workers, such as temporary regulars (*rinjiko*), non-committed temporary regulars, day labourers, and extra workers (*shagaiko*) rarely enjoy the benefits of this concept.

So, those who join a company in a certain recruitment year, by and large, progress up the organization in almost the same time frame. Eventually, the ones more competent (or seen by *manejimento* as more competent or more diligent) would rise to *shacho* or *kaicho* (president or chairman), but that involves a lot of intra-company politics, give and take and a large dose of personal ambition. For the most part, the Japanese corporation remains a pyramidal base of younger 'maturing' juniors, a middle rung of experienced *jichos* and *kyokuchos* (similar to a joint director and divisional director in Western companies) and finally on top, those headed to the Board.

The system of *nenko joretsu* hides many a crack of inefficiency and sometimes even corporate lethargy. Sometimes, deadwood ends up smothering go-getters. But, in the overall assessment, it seems to work, and work well.

19

RINGI SEIDO

Ringi seido is the 'written proposal system' that defines Japanese bureaucracy.

If there is one thing common between India and Japan, and perhaps most Commonwealth countries, it is the penchant for the written word.

The *ringi sho* in Japanese is the 'written proposal document', which is very similar to the 'note for approval' (NFA) initiated every single day in every other government or corporate office. As the NFAs accumulate into a 'file', it begins to become very similar to the *ringi seido* way in Japan, or the 'written proposal system'.

The *ringi* is initiated by the concerned department or division within the company and circulated to other departments and divisions, across hierarchies. It needs to navigate its way through many and multiple layers of management. Respective managers need to affix their stamp of approval to the document with their *hanko* (a name seal) in the appropriate place. If a manager disagrees with the *ringi*, he affixes his *hanko* either at a slant or upside down, signifying dissent or conditional acceptance. And should a manager completely disagree, then he passes the document on to the next person in the chain without stamping his *hanko*.

The smooth passage of the *ringi* actually depends on the negotiating skills of the initiating manager, as also his ability to call in favours, invoke seniors to lend their weight and support to the document and consistent follow-up across layers of management, horizontally and vertically.

It is also important to understand some related terminology. The term *hourensou* refers to frequent and timely reporting, staying ever-connected and having constant discussions – all deemed necessary attributes for collaboration and the flow of information within the Japanese corporate culture. Similarly, *hou* stands for *houkoku*, the Japanese word for 'reporting'. Another related word, *ren,* comes from *renraku*, the word for 'informing'. Last, but not least, is the word *sou,* which is derived from *soudan*, the word for 'consulting'. This refers to 'getting your hands dirty', to identify or solve immediate problems and leaders are not exempt from this. Aspects of these principles are often mistaken by Western managers to be 'micromanagement', but these are essentially the ingredients that help make *ringi seido* a success.

How *ringi seido*-driven companies work depends on internal culture. Any project of consequence requires sufficient lubrication of the *ringi seido* system, especially where financials are involved. Since, the *ringi* may require a lot of *nemawashi* (consensus building, or, more appropriately, watering of the roots), the entire process requires a highly developed sense of vigilance, patience and perseverance.. The outsider may never really know where the *ringi* has reached, or if it is stuck. But the internal organization fully understands the obstructions as well as the objections. The progress remains 'bottom up' and there is really no way to push a 'top-down' approval. The *ringi* almost has a life of its own. It goes through many rounds of approvals at multiple levels, each with its own level of difficulty (and sometimes even treachery) and yet, may not make it to the final sign-off. Japanese bureaucracy can make the old British masters look like yesterday's novices!

20

SENPAI KŌHAI

Senpai kōhai in Japanese actually defines a 'senior-junior' relationship.

Senpai ('earlier colleague') and *kōhai* ('later colleague') are terms that describe an informal hierarchical interpersonal relationship found in organizations, associations, clubs, businesses, and schools in Japan. The concept is based on the tenets of Japanese philosophy and *senpai kōhai* relationships are deeply rooted in Japanese society.

The relationship is an interdependent one, as a *senpai* requires a *kōhai* and vice versa, and *senpai kōhai* establishes a bond that is determined by the date of entry to an organization. The *kōhai* defers to the *senpai*'s seniority and experience, and speaks to the *senpai* using honorific language: *sonkeigo* (respectful language), *kenjogo* (humble language) and *teineigo* (polite language). Tonality of language is a very important component of the *senpai kōhai* relationship. A *senpai*, for example, always addresses a *kōhai* with the suffix *-kun* after the *kōhai*'s given name or surname, regardless of gender. A *kōhai* similarly addresses a *senpai* with the suffix *-senpai* or *-san*; similarly it is extremely unusual for a *kōhai* to refer to a *senpai* with the suffix *-sama*, which symbolizes the highest level of respect for the person being spoken to.

Japan being *tate shakai*, or a 'vertical society', the Japanese have a strong sense of hierarchical relations. Besides the hierarchical titles in the organization they belong to, senior-junior relations by age are considered important. This probably comes from the Confucian influence imported from China way back in their history. But it remains an important influence even today.

The *senpai kōhai* decorum is followed even when a boss, junior in age, speaks to a subordinate senior in years. The boss will speak to such an older subordinate with much respect even though the subordinate reports to him. Which is why when seeing anyone for the first time, the Japanese try to confirm in advance whether this person is senior or junior to them, in order to decide what kind of language they need to use.

The *senpai-kōhai* relationship is the cornerstone in interpersonal relations within the Japanese business world too; for example, at meetings the lower-level employee should sit in the seat closest to the door, called *shimoza* ('lower seat'), while the senior employee (sometimes the boss) sits next to some important guest in a position called *kamiza* ('upper seat').

These *senpai-kōhai* relationship rules apply not only within any particular organization but permeate through the entire society. Once Japanese children enter junior high school, they start calling the students in the higher classes 'senpai' and the students in the lower classes 'kōhai'. Younger ones pay respect to and do all kinds of chores for the older ones, while older ones, in return, help and take care of the younger ones.

Senpai kōhai relations between the graduates of famous universities are especially strong and influential. Sometimes, this is called *gakubatsu*, or 'school clique'. The hidden networks of *senpai-kōhai* are spread all around, inside and outside organizations. These can be very helpful, but at the same time, they can be dangerous. You could sometimes be privy to important information or be introduced to a helpful person through this network. On the flip side, a negative impression made at some stage can also be communicated very quickly to one and all.

21

SHA CHIKU

❧

Sha Chiku simply means 'corporate sheep' or 'corporate livestock'. Japan is a nation defined and dominated by herd syndrome that is not quite seen anywhere else in the world. But specifically, in this case, this herd is of 'lifers' employed by large Japanese corporations. A regimented, disciplined, and wholly committed cadre of employees who live and die for the job.

Said to have been conceived by Satoshi Azuchi (1937–), novelist and chairman of the Japan Supermarket Association – who was himself loaned to the Summit chain of supermarkets from the Sumitomo Corporation, which is one of the largest trading companies in Japan – and popularized by the journalist Makoto Sataka (1945–), who extended the thought of 'corporate sheep' to 'corporate slavery', a life time of subservience and corporate bondage.

To understand this uniquely Japanese concept, one perhaps first needs to understand *shu-shinkoyo,* lifetime employment, that the Japanese corporations created post the Second World War. It was a two-way commitment: lifetime employment guaranteed by the corporation, and lifetime loyalty reciprocated by the employee.

But, to be fair, such herd-like behaviour has, in fact, been a conspicuous part of life in Japan for centuries. The Japanese were conditioned intellectually, emotionally and physically to conform to a highly refined etiquette system and to function as a member of a group rather than as an individual. Eventually, this group mentality became the norm. This group behaviour is most eloquently expressed in the *jidai geki,* or period films, depicting life from the seventeenth through to the nineteenth centuries.

To illustrate the depth of commitment, it would be good to share a story told by a young Japanese corporate manager from a small-town named Kamaishi, where he grew up. His father, his uncle and a cousin were all employed at a Nippon Steel plant. By the late '80s, Nippon Steel, the world's largest steelmaker, kept the factory operating long after it became unprofitable and closed it only gradually, transferring workers to other plants. When it could no longer transfer workers, the company scrambled to create almost any business it could to employ the former steelworkers there, including an ill-fated attempt at growing mushrooms. The result: former steelworkers are now involved in businesses from truck bodies and office furniture to growing miniature Brazilian orchids, as well as making meat substitutes from soy protein. The young manager's sixty-year-old old father still works for Nippon Steel, only now he sells imitation bologna made from soybeans rather than operating a huge blast furnace.

This laudable commitment for life has, however, had its downside too. The large corporations (even government organizations) have for years tried to create and maintain uniformity, conformity, rules, symbols, customs and rituals, really a codified corporate hymn sheet, such that all employees behave at all times in a very defined and similar way.

Individuality is curbed. Mavericks are frowned upon. Any interests or hobbies outside the company are discouraged. Falling out of line can lead to serious ostracization.

The entire work force thus starts to resemble a mass of corporate sheep.

Post the Bubble in the 90s, much has started to change. Much will change. But the employee-sheep still remain yoked to corporate discipline, loyalty and harmony.

22

SOKUSENRYOKU

Sokusenryoku translates into 'ready fire power' or 'battle-ready forces' that are an immediate asset (to a team or firm), or someone who can be a prompt and efficient player for the team or the company.

Sokusenryoku is very similar to the HR concept of 'lateral recruitment', which is the process of hiring an 'expert' for a vacancy that needs to be filled from another organization that is a recognized leader in the field.

In the good old days of lifetime employment and the seniority system in Japan, once a person entered the company or joined the government as a fresh college graduate, his employment for life was practically guaranteed. Those who were recruited in the same year (*douki*) were promoted and their salaries raised almost simultaneously until they reached a certain age when some were chosen to become top managers and the rest had to retire. A younger person to be promoted ahead of his senior colleagues was an exception. Usually, the younger person, regardless of how capable he had proven himself, had to wait for his turn until the senior colleague retired or was promoted to a higher position.

Under such a system, employees were expected to nurture their loyalty to the company. It was only in rare cases that a person was recruited from outside the company in the middle of his career, not to mention from a rival company, since such a move would interfere with the underlying conformity of the system.

But, Japan is changing.

Under the influence of globalization and increasing competition, job hopping has become more common in Japan. The Japanese mid-career job market may still not be as dynamic as elsewhere, but it's expanding more than ever. And *sokusenryoku*, or 'immediate reinforcement', has become the buzzword of recruitment marketing.

It is accepted in Japan that it takes up to three years and a cost of around 16 million Yen to train a new college graduate to become a business asset. But if a company were to hire an already matured specialist, he would pump up the workforce immediately and, even at a higher salary, could actually be a cheaper option.

One of the main reasons for the need for *sokusenryoku* is the greater demand for specialized skills across companies. An advertising agency needing to reinforce its new content business may, for example, want to recruit a trained domain resource from a movie distributor or a broadcast company. Similarly, the marketing department of a growing company may want to have an in-house advertising expert. Or, the finance department of a large manufacturer may want a treasury expert on its team. As it is, IT specialists are being recruited externally by most companies as this is a skill set that is of recent origin, and the demands of this domain change very rapidly. For many Japanese companies, *sokusenryoku* is the only practical solution.

But the phenomenon does not come without its attendant problems. In the still homogeneous Japanese corporate culture, these mid-career entrants often experience a hard time merging with the new environment. Transplantation is obviously not easy.

23

TANSHIN FUNIN

Tanshin funin is best described as 'persons on assignment alone', but the closest interpretation of the term is actually 'bachelor husbands', jokingly also referred to as *chongas*.

According to the national census, there were 7,26,000 workers living alone, away from their families, in 2010. The figure has been consistently growing from 3,34,000 in 1980.

'Bachelor husbands' or 'business bachelors', leaving the family behind to get ahead in their profession, is a phenomenon in a country whose business is growing both domestically and internationally. Naturally, this has had its impact on the institution of the family. 'Absent Fathers, Feminized Sons, Selfish Mothers and Disobedient Daughters' was the assessment of the Japan Policy Research Institute on the *tanshin funin* situation some years ago. But this may actually be somewhat of an exaggeration.

For a Japanese worker, it is difficult to say 'no' when assigned to a job far away from his city of residence. If married, especially with school-going children, the decision invariably is not to uproot the family, but for the man of the house to take up the assignment in the new city alone. Hence, the terms 'bachelor husbands' or 'business bachelors'.

Tanshin funin is perhaps the ultimate form of 'paternal nurturance' and sacrifice to care for one's family, and it hits middle-aged men disproportionately. Common hazards of being a *tanshin funin* are loneliness, poor mental health, poor diet and excessive drinking. Some also engage in extra-marital affairs, or patronize prostitutes. There is, however, a surprisingly high degree of tolerance for these practices among *tanshin funin* wives: 43 per cent stated that the separation did not damage their marriage, compared to the 20 per cent who confessed anxiety over the extended separation. Of course, this may reveal a 'response bias' since Japanese women are traditionally not supposed to complain, and the custom of *gaman* (grin and bear it) is instilled in them from a young age. But it may also be possible that except for needing their husbands' pay cheques, Japanese women find *tanshin funin* much less stressful than men do.

Actually, it may not necessarily be a bad thing to live away from the family for some time. For the husband, moving to a smaller town, or overseas, could mean a lot of time saved every day compared to the daily commute to and in Tokyo, allowing more time to dabble in their hobbies. Also, the separation leads perhaps to the realization of how much value the wife brings to the family unit. And this then leads to savouring their time together as a couple, making for a more enduring husband–wife bond. For the wife, too, as a famous commercial put it, 'it's best to have a healthy husband out of home'.

But this separation, while allowing time and space between the spouses, has also led to divorce in some cases. Some divorces have occurred because the husband had an affair; or some, because the wife with the husband not around, found pleasure elsewhere.

Whatever may it be, as long as *uchi no kaisha* (the internal, familial world of the company) persists, where the employer rules over the family, *tanshin funin* will remain a reality Japan has to bear with.

24

UMA NO MIMI NI NENBUTSU

Uma no mimi ni nenbutsu means whispering *nenbutsu* – a prayer to the Buddha – into the horse's ear.

It means sharing your knowledge with someone who does not really like it. *Nenbutsu* is the Buddhist chant '*Namu Amida Butsu*'. But *uma no mimi ni nenbutsu* is closer in meaning to a wasted effort; dangling pearls before a swine.

Those who do business with Japan will perhaps tell you that the Japanese business decision-making process is changing from the bottom-up style to top-down style in order to cope with the globalization of the country's business in recent years. But this is not necessarily true. It is not easy to change orientation and work habits, especially when they are so deeply ingrained in the culture of a nation.

Let's say, you want to promote a business opportunity to a Japanese company. You are lucky enough to have an acquaintance with this very important person in the top management. You make an appointment and give him a thorough presentation on the subject. But alas! After a few days, he will call you and introduce you to a 'person-in-charge' at the bottom of the organization. This 'person-in-charge' starts to work closely with you. It is his job from then on to prepare a thick document explaining why the proposal should be considered seriously, all the pros and cons attached to it in detail; he has to run around behind the scenes, among people in the organization who are related to the subject, to nurture a consensus, obtain approvals from various internal meetings to move up the ladder if the proposal finds favour. If you are lucky, the proposal may eventually reach the final decision-making committee at the very top.

All along, the 'person-in-charge' will keep asking you questions about the project; questioning and rechecking the most trivial of details during the course of the proposal finding its way up the organization; but his answers to your own questions on the progress of the matter or internal reactions will always be vague and evasive.

You eventually become frustrated and ask the 'person-in-charge' to see you in order to know what's actually going on. The 'person-in-charge' will most probably invite you to a fabulous restaurant and treat you to fabulous food. He will be nice and polite throughout the meal. But what's going on with your project will continue to remain vague. You come back as much in the dark as when you decided to ask to meet him in person.

More often than not, you will be left in a limbo for several months and eventually, will receive a polite rejection, perhaps an apology at the very end. So much for whispering *nenbutsu* into the horse's ear!

Uma no mimi ni nenbutsu is all about the lack of transparency in the Japanese corporate world. It is also about how access to the entire system is so very limited, and you may end up merely feeding a minor cog in the wheel, who eventually can neither influence a decision nor help you gain favour within the Japanese corporation. Foreigners doing business with Japan find this extremely frustrating and demeaning, but then, there is no better option.

II
____

AESTHETICS

25

ENSOU

Ensou refers to a circle that is hand-drawn in one continuous brushstroke. This is enabled when the mind is free and allows the body to create, that too in a single moment of time. This is a very powerful pillar of thought in Japanese creativity.

The *ensou* symbolizes absolute enlightenment, strength, elegance, the universe, and *mu* (the void). It manifests a minimalism born of Japanese Buddhist aesthetics.

Drawing *ensou* is a creative practice in Japanese ink painting called *sumi-e*. The tools and mechanics of drawing the *ensou* are the same as those used in traditional Japanese calligraphy: use of a brush (*fude*) to apply ink to *washi* (a thin Japanese paper).

The *ensou* circle may be open or closed. The open circle is deemed as 'incomplete', allowing for movement, development, innovation as well as the imperfection of all things. Zen practitioners relate this idea to the popular concept of *wabi-sabi*, the beauty of imperfection.

When the circle is closed, it represents perfection. It stands for completion. It epitomizes closure and success. Fulfilment. Achievement.

Usually the *ensou* is drawn in one fluid, expressive stroke. The brushstroke is especially swift when drawn according to the *sousho* style of Japanese calligraphy. Once the *ensou* is drawn, it is never changed because it evidences the character of its creator and the context of its creation in a brief, contiguous period of time. Drawing *ensou* is a spiritual practice that one might perform as often as once per day.

This spiritual practice of drawing *ensou* or writing Japanese calligraphy for self-realization is called *hitsuzendou,* the 'way of the brush'. *Ensou* exemplifies the various dimensions of the *wabi-sabi:* both in perspective and aesthetic, *fukinsei,* or asymmetry, even-unevenness and irregularity, *kanso,* or simplicity (in fact, uncomplicatedness), *koko,* or basic/weather-beaten, *shizen,* or without any pretence and natural, *yuugen,* or subtly profound grace, *datsuzoku,* or freedom, and *seijaku,* or tranquillity.

Ensou, the zen circle, is about symbolizing the wholeness of the spirit, yet it symbolizes the void too. The eternal void driven by the quest for knowledge. Since the way you paint the *ensou* expresses eloquently the way your life is at that moment of time, the inherent message is to stay firmly inside here, so that nothing can shake or shatter you. Much like the comfort of the womb. Protective. Eternal. Infinite.

While art has always employed the concept of the *ensou* zen circle as an important building block, one can witness the application of the *ensou* in advertising and communications too. One can, for example, sit through a phenomenal presentation at the Suzuki headquarters in Hamamatsu, where one of the automobile designers explains the whole concept of using rounded contours in the design of car body parts to allow 'breathing space' in every nook and corner of the car, giving its owners the leeway to use the rounded 'residuality' in a personally comfortable and commodious way. Such intelligent use of space can then be put to good use. For example, in Japan, the Suzuki Wagon-R car has space created under the driver's seat for a shopping basket and in the boot for a mini ironing board and there is also an iron that the driver can use to smoothen out their jacket before an important engagement!

26

FUROSHIKI

*F*uroshiki is a wrapping cloth.

Wrapping is one practice the Japanese are very good at, and very proud of. One is amazed when one sees for the first time how neatly and quickly attendants at Japanese stores wrap up the things one just bought, using beautiful wrapping papers. As gifting is a national pastime, so to say, in Japan, wrapping the gifts to make them look increasingly attractive is equally an obsession. But it took many, many years for the current abundant supply and variety of wrapping papers to become as commonly available as they are today. Before that, there was just the *furoshiki*, or the wrapping cloth.

The word *furoshiki* can be divided into two parts: *furo* and *shiki*. *Furo* means bath. *Shiki* means mat. So till not very far back in time, the *furoshiki* was a common bath mat, no more. It was just a mundane tool for the Japanese folk to carry their change on the way to the public bath, wipe their feet after taking the bath, and come home carrying the laundry. Somewhere along the way, the *furoshiki* no longer came to be used as just a bath mat, and somehow, somewhere, all wrapping cloths started to be referred to as it. This practice most likely dates back to the Edo period (1603–1868 AD).

Thus, *furoshiki* over time became a chief multipurpose utility. It worked as a bag as well as a wrapping device. *Furoshiki* would come in various sizes, and with a large one you could even wrap and carry your sleeping mattress. While visitors carried their gifts wrapped in *furoshiki*, students carried their books, businessmen carried their papers and blue-collar workers carried their lunch boxes wrapped in it. Cash was put in an envelope and wrapped in a smaller *furoshiki* when given to someone. Women started using it instead of a purse when going out. Until this day, a stereotyped caricature of a thief always shows him carrying his loot in a big *furoshiki* around his neck!

However, in current times, since most of the wrappings are now done with paper, and most of the carrying is done in bags, the *furoshiki* has become a gift item to be bought and admired just for its pretty design. It comes dyed in printed patterns or with beautiful pictures. The most popular and time-honoured pattern of the *furoshiki* is the arabesque design of intertwined foliage printed in white over a green base. It is said that similar patterns have even been found in ancient Greek and Persian designs. No one knows how they travelled this far. And yes, the caricature thief referred below always carries a *furoshiki* of this design!

And, by the way, *ooburoshikiwohirogeru*, or 'spreading out a large *furoshiki*' means to boast about one's ambitious future plans bordering on fantasy. The Japanese mock people with such big egos by calling them *ooburoshiki*.

27

GEIDOU

The Japanese concept of *geidou* says that *the way* you do something is just as important as the result you achieve. It's the key to understanding how the Japanese think.

Geidou came to be associated with three different genres: classical theatre and performance, traditional crafts and techniques, and martial arts. In *geidou*, studying the ethics, morals and the etiquette upon which these arts are based is a mental exercise that is as important as studying the techniques. As such, following the philosophy of *geidou* means the sharpening of your mind, as well as the honing of your skills.

Japanese martial arts, for example, are always described with a 'the way ...' description, like in *kendou* – *the way* of the sword, *aikiduo* – *the way* of life energy, and *judou* – *the* gentle *way*. Similarly 'the way ...' is also a common descriptor in Japanese traditional arts: *sadou* – *the way* of tea (tea ceremony), *kadou* – *the way* of flowers (*ikebana* flower arrangement) and *shodou* – *the way* of the brush (Japanese calligraphy).

Western arts are usually defined by their end result. An Impressionist painting would be an Impressionist painting, no matter how the artist went about painting it. In Japanese arts, the opposite is sometimes the case – *the way* the art was created is as important as who painted what, or when. This is called *geidou* (the way of art).

Geidou embodies the spirit of discipline and ethics. Interestingly, the character for *gei,* as in *geisha,* is the same as in *geidou.* The level of commitment, the discipline and the ethic in not only the work but also the life of a *geisha* exemplifies the gravity and importance of *geidou.* Similarly, martial arts warriors followed *geidouron,* or the *geidou* theory, through a systemized regimen called *kata,* or the form. The journey is as important, in fact more important, than the destination. If the journey is undertaken *the way* it is prescribed, the destination will be but naturally attained. All of these arts and art forms are tacit communications and it is the appreciation of this dimension that is of paramount importance. Japanese martial arts are not about just defeating the enemy. They're about the path that gets you there. In a tea ceremony, often considered the best example of *geidou,* the cup of tea is trivial compared to the process of making, serving and consuming the tea. The process is the art. It is the beauty. The *geidou.*

Geidou can be seen in the way Japanese people think. The Japanese never encourage shortcuts. There is no incentive in quick wins. *The way,* the right way, the real way should always be followed, step-by-step. Always. Yes, always.

Geidou remains as relevant in modern-day Japan, and in modern-day business. When dealing with Japanese businesses, it is of vital importance to know that it is not just the business but the way business is conducted that is equally important. If you follow the due process, the end result is likely to be positive.

28

HAIKU

The term *haiku* is derived from the first element of the word *haikai*, which is a humorous form of *renga* – a linked-verse poem – and the second element of the word *hokku* (the initial stanza of a *renga*). *Haiku* is an unrhymed seventeen-syllable verse, arranged in three lines of five, seven and five syllables. Despite its succinct form, it contains the essence of the Japanese people's aesthetics, view of nature, philosophy, thought, and sentiments.

This short form of Japanese poetry has some essential qualities. One of its important facets is *kire*, often represented by the juxtaposition of two images or ideas. The *kire* have a *kireji*, or 'cutting word', between them as a kind of verbal punctuation mark that signals the movement of separation and impacts the manner in which the juxtaposed elements are related. The poem also has a seasonal reference, *kigo*, usually drawn from a *saijiki*, an extensive but defined list of such terms.

Initially called *hokku*, which set the tone of a *renga*, it had to mention in its three lines subjects such as the season, time of day, and the dominant features of the landscape, giving it almost the form of an independent poem. *Hokku* was first referred to as *haiku* by the Japanese writer Masaoka Shiki at the end of the nineteenth century.

Composing a *haiku* means giving a voice to the 'other' and taking a slice of life. By doing so, one can tap into the cosmic source of earth's life, and create synchronicity with other living beings. This is also a process of self-discovery, a journey to the depths of one's own heart. It is through the 'other' that one discovers things about oneself. *Haiku* is not merely looking at beautiful scenes of nature from afar, but stepping into their midst, and appreciating them up close and on their own terms.

Why has *haiku* been so popular as a form of poetry in Japan? First, because *haiku* is short and has the fixed form of five–seven–five Japanese syllables, it is more accessible. Longer and freestyle poems are more difficult to write and read. Second, *haiku* is predominantly a poetry of seasons. The theme of a *haiku* is almost fixed, hence it is easier to find a subject for *haiku*, such as a slight shift in seasons or seasonal life, and there is really no need to add any emotional interpretation to express it. Third, because a *haiku* is short, it is easy to remember. Fourth, it appeals to the innate sense of discipline and uniformity so desired by the Japanese.

Haiku is popular the world over because it imparts the most important lesson that writers must learn: show, don't tell. *Haiku's* grounding in a single moment teaches writers to narrow their compositions to only those sensory elements that are critical to the scene without unnecessary commentary. This dictates a habit of close observation, coupled with a brevity of form, which disciplines writers to choose adjectives and verbs that convey the message most powerfully. *Haiku* encourages writers to create more interesting compositions based on demonstration or 'showing' what is happening rather than merely 'telling' the reader.

29

IKI, MIYABI AND WABI-SABI

Iki in Japanese is an aesthetic expression of simplicity, sophistication, spontaneity, and originality. It is supposedly ephemeral, romantic, straightforward, measured, audacious, and smart. Nurtured in the plebeian culture of the Edo period, *iki* is not overly refined, pretentious or complicated; it is also not showy, slick, coquettish, or, generally, cute. *Iki* may exhibit any of these traits in a smart, direct, and unabashed manner: sometimes best expressed as a combination of 'boiling intuition and exploding improvisation'.

Miyabi is also a traditional Japanese aesthetic ideal, but usually translated as 'elegance' or 'refinement'. It has its roots in the aristocratic culture of the Heian period.

Iki is effervescent, but more common and more colloquial. More chic. Modern-day Japanese stylistically live more in the *iki* mould: a lifestyle that is smart and savvy. This is reflected in their daily fashion, their choice of food, entertainment and socializing, such that *iki*-ness becomes almost a part of their body language and comfort.

Miyabi, in contrast, is about embellishing manners, diction, and feelings to eliminate all roughness and crudity so as to achieve the highest grace. *Miyabi* is the complete opposite of the rustic and the crude.

Wabi-Sabi is aligned to both *iki* and *miyabi*. It comes from the aesthetical concept of Zen Buddhism, typically seen in the tea ceremony. *Wabi-Sabi* stands for simple, subtle, and unobtrusive beauty. In the Japanese context, it is an enriched, subdued appearance or experience of intrinsically fine quality with economy of form, line, and effort, producing a timeless tranquillity. *Wabi-Sabi* objects appear to be simple overall, but they include subtle details, such as textures, that balance simplicity with complexity.

Iki, miyabi and *wabi-sabi* collectively represent the very evolved and elevated Japanese mindset regarding aesthetics and design. There are shades and shades of subtle differentiation. Shades of fine detail. Shades of cultural context. Every expression, every mood is different. It is also the Japanese ability to absorb and internalize these varied, yet connected concepts that are philosophical and practical at the same time.

Wabi-Sabi in Japan has come to denote those things that exhibit in paradox and, all at once, the very best of everything and nothing: Elegant simplicity. Effortless effectiveness. Understated excellence. Beautiful imperfection.

It is not easy to always understand the fine nuances of these different measures of Japanese aesthetics and thinking. They are concepts that are distinct, yet intertwined in the Japanese mind. The beauty of these concepts is that they are actually practised and propagated in daily life. Perfection and imperfection are equally sought and accepted. There is beauty in both. In fact, it is the understanding of imperfection that leads to the understanding of perfection. To us non-Japanese, it is best not to wrestle with concepts such as *iki*, *miyabi* and *wabi-sabi*, but to take them at face value, and move on.

30

JO-HA-KYŪ

At its simplest *Jo-ha-kyū* means 'beginning, middle, end'.

Jo-ha-kyū is an ancient term originating in *Noh* theatre. It first appeared in the fourteenth-century writings of the master Zeami Motokiyo, who used it to describe the development of story and action in *Noh* drama. In theatre, music, and literature, *Jo-ha-kyū* encapsulates the idea, in the simplest terms, of a beginning, middle and an end.

The characters with which *Jo-ha-kyū* is written, however, provide much more meaning than just 'beginning, middle, end'. While '*jo*' commonly does mean 'beginning', '*ha*' and '*kyū*' have much larger meanings. '*Ha*' on its own can be read as '*yaburu*', which means to tear, break or crack. '*Kyū*' means 'sudden, rapid, urgent, emergency'. These meanings for '*ha*' and '*kyū*' give a very different feel to the idea of '*Jo-ha-kyū*'. All of these meanings, when juxtaposed with the basal idea of 'beginning, middle and end', provide a feeling of tension or stress, beginning and building to a moment when the tension breaks into action, the resolution of which brings us to the end.

Jo-ha-kyū is theorized on modulation and movement, as applied to a wide variety of traditional Japanese arts. This concept is applied to elements of the tea ceremony, to *kendou* and other martial arts, and to traditional theatre. The concept finds its origin in *gagaku* court music, specifically in the manner in which elements of the music are distinguished and described. Though eventually fused into a variety of disciplines, it was most famously adapted, and perhaps most thoroughly studied and discussed, by the great *Noh* playwright Zeami as mentioned above, who viewed it as a universal concept, applying it to the patterns of movement of all things.

In *gagaku*, where the term originated, *jo-ha-kyū* was not generally cited as a single term, but as three separate terms, referring to possible portions of musical pieces which might be arranged in different ways to form a complete piece. *Jo* sections were the introductory sections, proceeding in a calm and placid manner, and lacking a predetermined rhythmic scheme. *Ha* sections proceeded at a measured pace and featured a set rhythmic scheme. *Kyū* sections possessed a faster tempo and a set rhythmic scheme. It was not necessary to include all three, *jo*, *ha*, and *kyū* sections, for a *gagaku* piece to be considered a complete performance piece.

It is perhaps in the theatre that *jo-ha-kyū* is used the most extensively on most levels. Following the writings of Zeami, all major forms of Japanese traditional drama (*Noh*, *Kabuki*, and *Jōruri*) utilize the concept of *jo-ha-kyū*: from the choice and arrangement of plays across a performance day to the composition and pacing of acts within the play, and even down to the individual actions of the actors.

There is another dimension too to *jo-ha-kyū* which suggests rising acceleration. When drawing a sword for a *nukitsuke* cut, the *iaidoka* commences the draw slowly, that too with a relaxed grip. As the sword is drawn, the speed is increased and the grip becomes firmer (but not tighter) until the sword is free. Once free, the *iaidoka* snaps the *monouchi* of the sword towards the target by tightening her grip. The *iaidoka's* grip then relaxes as she repositions her sword for the second cut of the *kata*, and the process of acceleration begins again.

31

KAKIJUN

Kakijun refers to the rules on properly writing *kanji* characters (logographic Chinese characters which are also a part of the Japanese system of writing), specifically in the order in which each stroke (traditionally rendered in paintbrush *sumi-ink*) must be written.

The premise is that if you mess up the order, then it's entirely wrong even if it looks like it had been written in the correct order.

Kakijun is something that could have significance only in Japan.

It highlights the essential importance of process as opposed to results.

If it's not done the right way, it's wrong.

Japanese society emphasizes the Zen-like spiritual virtue of what is happening within the individual and not just the Western-style pragmatism of getting things done, making money or winning status.

In another sense, *kakijun* is about fixating on regulations, not for the sake of appearances, but for the substance of the action.

Kakijun penalizes deviations, discourages creativity and rewards conformity. Yet, *kakijun* can be a beautiful concept. Because, as a process, it is defined, disciplined and rigorous.

Most times, in fact, Japanese calligraphy almost looks like abstract Western art. It is forceful. It is the artist's individuality expressed in art form. It is in fact evidence of how Japanese art is actually defined as the beauty of the process.

Japanese rules of everyday etiquette, about how to enter a door, how to bow, how to drink tea, and more are almost like a choreographed dance. How to do something in everyday life is part of the definition of a person's individual value as a human being, as a subset of Japanese society. Pretty deep thinking, isn't that!

The biggest learning from *kakijun* is the fundamental appreciation of the importance of process, and the adherence to rules and systems. This has been one of the strongest glues in keeping Japanese society together and getting every individual to march, even in things most mundane, to a common drumbeat. This therefore has become the essence of their harmony, even their punctuality, as everything happens as it is planned to happen and is both predictable and controllable. This also contributes, perhaps in big measure, to everything in Japan looking so clean and orderly. There is no scope and no allowance for individual or impromptu decision making. Hence, there are no surprises, no deviations.

It may be stretching the point too far, but many Western thinkers attribute many of Japan's world-beating manufacturing processes to initial learnings and discipline imbibed at a very early age in school in following *kakijun*, both in form and in spirit. No shortcuts. No jumping the gun. An ingrained philosophy of doing things right. Always right. And, this has, over time, also become the foundation of rigorous quality control in Japanese manufacturing.

Basically, when the process becomes the hymn sheet, quality is bound to follow.

Kakijun is also of paramount importance because its practice, day in and day out, leads to perfection. And therein lies the infallibility of the concept that practice makes perfect. Especially when processes are at the heart of that practice and that perfection.

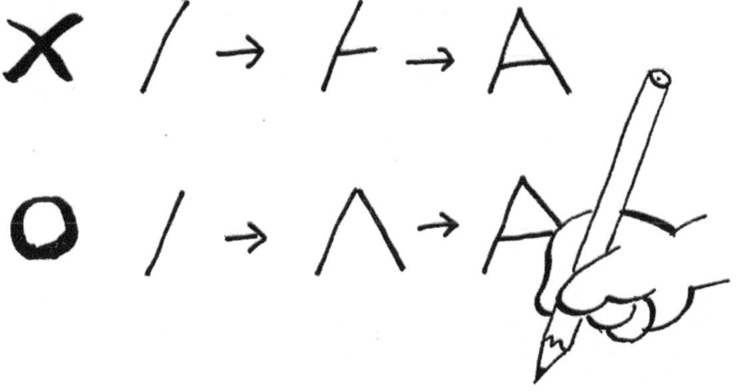

32

KAWAII

Kawaii in Japanese means lovable, cute or adorable.

The word *kawaii* comes from a phrase that means 'a radiant face', actually the blushing of an embarrassed person. Over time, the meaning metamorphosed to the modern word 'cute', while the way it is written in the Japanese alphabet actually means 'able to be loved'. *Kawaii* has become almost all-pervasive, finding its way into all forms of popular Japanese culture, entertainment, clothing, food, toys, personal appearance, behaviour and even mannerisms.

Since its very beginnings, the *kawaii* craze has been a kind of rebellion against the seriousness of adulthood – a counter-balance to the harsh realities of the real world.

This culture of 'cute' began in the 1970s with a movement pioneered by teenage girls, involving handwriting in a childlike style. The new script earned itself a variety of names, such as *marui ji* (round writing), *koneko ji* (kitten writing), and *burikko ji* (fake-child writing), and showed text with stylized lines, hearts, stars, Latin characters, and cartoon faces. The pursuit of *kawaii* enabled the youth to find a sense of individuality and playfulness in an increasingly serious and depersonalized environment. While many schools initially banned this writing style, advertisers quickly latched onto the trend, using the new aesthetic to market products to younger customers.

In 1974, the stationary company Sanrio launched the character Hello Kitty, printing the now-iconic whiskered white cat on a vinyl coin purse. Forty years later, Hello Kitty has reportedly been placed on over 50,000 products, including toaster ovens, alarm clocks, airplanes, and even sex toys, in more than seventy countries. In 2008, Japan named Hello Kitty as its global tourism ambassador. It was almost an official invite to the rest of the world to join in on the adorability binge of *kawaii*.

The Japanese concept of *kawaii* has grown from a national trend to a global phenomenon. Sanrio's Hello Kitty has been valued at an astonishing $7 billion; the Oxford English Dictionary, in fact, named an emoji its 2015 Word of the Year; and Nintendo's Pokémon Go recently became the most-downloaded game in smartphone history. The *kawaii* movement is wide in scope, spanning Manga comics, Harajuku fashion, and Takashi Murakami's 'Superflat' artworks, and more.

Kawaii creatures, by definition, have limited facial features – usually two wide eyes, a small nose, and maybe a dot for the mouth – rendering them emotionally abstruse and enabling viewers to interpret them through a personal prism. Almost always outlined in black, *kawaii* characters are mostly pastel-coloured, graphically simple, and almost childlike in appearance. Designed to provoke a sense of nostalgia, they usually feature big heads and small bodies in order to match the proportions of infants and baby animals.

In today's Japanese culture, *kawaii* is expressed in myriad ways. Women and men actively partake of the culture of cuteness. Men shave their legs to mimic a teenage look, while singers and actors often sport longer hair. Japanese women prefer the 'cute look' of a 'childish round face' with large eyes signifying innocence. In fact, some women attempt to change the size of their eyes by wearing large contact lenses, large eyelash extensions, strong eye makeup and some even surgically modify their eyelids.

The *kawaii* syndrome in Japan has ensured that 'cute' and 'neat' have effectively displaced the former 'politically correct' Japanese aesthetics of 'beautiful' and 'refined'. In fact 'cute' *kawaii* is the magic term that encompasses everything that is acceptable and desirable in Japan now.

33

KEI-HAKU-TAN-SHOU

❧

Kei-Haku-Tan-Shou literally means light-slim-short-small. Miniaturization best describes the Japanese penchant for *kei-haku-tan-shou*. Japan is a small country. Japanese homes are small. Space is at a premium everywhere. The typical Japanese urban denizen takes trains to nearly everywhere, and may, most times, not even own a car. This means that anything they carry around with them needs to be light and compact. Small living spaces also demand economy and practicality of design.

Seeking minimality is not new to the Japanese. For generations, Japanese artisans endeavoured to create everything as small, as concise and as precise as they could make any object or product. Without sacrificing either beauty or aesthetics, the objective was to use minimum material and minimum space; in fact, maximum value, maximum engineering, maximum benefit in the minimum size.

This minimization mindset went into overdrive post the Second World War as Japanese industry excelled in creating products that were high on technology and portability, but light-slim-short-small in size. This was more so with consumer electronics and household appliances. The Japanese pioneered the concept of 'compact' in music, from radios to transistors to Walkmans, making music easy to carry and keep. The same economy of size was applied to cameras. Every reduction in size was matched by equal or more refinement in technology and applications.

In a manner of speaking, *kei-haku-tan-shou* became the Japanese mantra for innovation. Much emphasis was put on 'light', which meant a lot of research into materials and forms that would result in lightweight products. This automatically helped in easier portability and, most times, reduced material costs. Slim-short-small dictated designers to work on making products easier to pick, handle and carry. This led to a lot of work on ergonomics, styling and 'palm-ability', which meant whether the product fitted well in the palm of the hand.

The Japanese penchant for *kei-haku-tan-shou* may also have been dictated by their need to carry around things. In America, except in a few metropolitan areas, the car is the preferred mode of conveyance. In Japan, most times you walk. And you carry the burden of your personal possessions. So, the lighter-slimmer-shorter-smaller they are, the better.

Kei-haku-tan-shou has been the most visible catalyst to the success of products on the *Hitto Shouhin Banzuke,* the hit products and services ranking list that is literally a trends Bible in Japan. The effort to smarten and miniaturize products led to, for example, the famous tamagotchi pets in the 1990s. To the uninitiated, tamagotchi is a handheld digital pet, housed in a small egg-shaped computer with an interface consisting of various buttons. The digital pets are equipped with a hunger metre, a happy metre, a discipline metre and programmed such that you can check age, weight and other body functions. Through the 1990s and early 2000s, the miniature pets became the biggest toy fad in the world with myriad innovations introduced with every new generation of the tamagotchi.

Kei-haku-tan-shou has been a major driver of Japanese global competitiveness. 'Small is beautiful' has become central to Japanese thinking over the last four or five decades, and has helped them create products across categories that look and feel great.

TAMAGOTCHI

34

NIKKI

Literally *Nikki* means 'diary'. This is sometimes also referred to as *Nikki Bungaku*, though this phrase is largely the creation of the twentieth century.

The Japanese have always loved to write diaries. An enormous number of diaries has been written depicting the everyday lives of people of different status in different times.

Diaries remain one of the most important genres in Japanese literature. Prominent works in this genre started to appear in the Heian period (794–1185 AD), when the aristocrats ruled the country. The world-famous *The Tale of Genji* was written during this era by a noblewoman named Murasaki Shikibu. Her diary called *Murasaki Shikibu Nikki* is a literary achievement acclaimed to this day. *Tosa Nikki*, *Kagerou Nikki*, *Izumi Shikibu Nikki* and *Sarashina Nikki* are a few prominent publications by other authors from the same period. In June 2013, *Midokanpakuki*, the original handwritten diary of Fujiwara No Michinaga (966–1027 AD), the most influential aristocrat of the time, was registered in UNESCO's Memory of the World. Other such registrations include the Magna Carta, Gutenberg Bible and a handwritten score by Beethoven.

Initially a favourite of the upper classes, the habit of writing diaries gradually trickled down to other sections of society over time. In the Edo period (1603–1868 AD) when peace reigned for over two-and-a-half centuries and the literacy rate surged, even regular townsfolk started to write diaries. It has now become a very important task for Japanese historians to study the enormous volume of diaries the Japanese people have left behind.

Donald Keene, the highly admired scholar of Japanese literature, was working as an intelligence officer during the Pacific War. One of his tasks was to translate the confiscated diaries of Japanese soldiers into English. He says he learned a lot about the Japanese by reading those diaries. He adds, 'In other countries, diaries are no more than reference material, but in Japan, there is a whole genre of literature dedicated to them. I think this is found only in Japanese literature.'

In Japan, diaries have always attempted to be an 'expression of the self', as opposed to a 'search for the self'. For example, in writing her *Kagero Nikki*, Mother of Michitsuna claims one motive to write the diary was 'to answer, should anyone ask, what is it like, the life of a married woman, that too, to a highly placed man?'

In current times, the Japanese people blog a lot on the internet. Blogs are not exactly like diaries, but their explosive expansion as a genre has perhaps something to do with this diary-loving tradition for sure. In fact, a major characteristic of the Japanese blogs, compared to those of other countries, is that they resemble diaries.

Also, these days, most Japanese celebrities use blogs for their PR and publicity. But in recent times, many celebrity blogs have backfired. This may be so because the literary style of writing a diary is so natural to them that they tend to forget that they are speaking to the public through the blog!

35

SHITSUKE, SEIRI, SEITON, SEIKETSU AND SEISOU

Shitsuke, seiri, seiton, seiketsu and *seisou* were the Famous Five or the 'Five-S' that revolutionized Japan in the 1970s, triggering a societal change that put the country onto the trajectory of hyper-growth. The Famous Five were the essential mantras that defined the Japanese approach to work, enshrined in a workplace that was akin to a place of worship.

Shitsuke means 'training', *seiri* means 'orderliness', *seiton* means 'neatness', *seiketsu* means 'cleanliness' and *seisou* means 'dustfree'.

These work ethics continue to define the Japanese orientation to their everyday work routine, where certain basics remain non-negotiable. The obsession with orderliness, cleanliness and neatness is almost equivalent to a national paranoia. Every Japanese has this training deeply ingrained in their minds.

One's experience with the Five-S approach does not have to start on the shop floor of a Japanese manufacturing unit. Japanese factories and workshops are spic and span. That goes without saying. But even in the office, working with Japanese expatriates, one can notice the high level of commitment to orderliness in day-to-day work. Every one of these expats carries a small pocket-size diary. This diary, with its neat Japanese annotations, not only contains the appointments of the day but also has meticulous notes of every meeting attended through the day.

Every document being readied for a client has hours of work poured into it, not just for content, but for a certain orderliness of thought. One marvels at the neat presentation style where every element of a job is broken up into component tasks, which in turn are allocated to a team or person, with deadlines set for review and closure. It is not that any of this is rocket science or stuff that no one else can do intuitively, but for the Japanese, the concept of Five-S is so deeply embedded in their psyche that doing things methodically and sequentially is just pure natural.

A friend of mine was on one of his first visits to a Japanese factory, that of Suzuki at Hamamatsu. This must have been around 1994 or 1995. Suzuki is much smaller than a Toyota or a Honda factory. But the operating principles are really the same, big or small. The Suzuki factory was neater than my friend's mother's kitchen. Every machine was scrubbed clean. The floor was scrubbed clean. Every worker wore his uniform, his helmet and his gloves without exception. So much so, that each one of them looked scrubbed clean! The gardens outside the factory were aesthetic, but, most importantly, there was not even a single leaf littering the grass. The staff canteen where he ate lunch was again almost antiseptically clean. He was escorted to meet O. Suzuki, the president of the company. The room was spartan, but, again, picture-book perfect.

Concepts like *kanban* (just-in-time delivery) and *kaizen* (continuous improvement) have received a lot of attention outside Japan for the innovative thinking they espouse. They denote radical new thinking the Western world has not seen. *Shitsuke, seiri, seiton, seiketsu* and *seisou* are equally serious as concepts, only not as well publicized or as well known. But these concepts are the basic building blocks of the Japanese obsession with quality, which starts with cleanliness.

36

WABI-SABI

The term *Wabi* traces its origin to *wa*, which refers to harmony, peace, tranquillity, and balance. *Sabi* by itself means 'the bloom of time'.

Wabi-Sabi is the Japanese art of finding beauty in humility, imperfection and profundity in nature. This art accepts the natural cycle of growth and death. It celebrates and toasts life's cracks; it also celebrates all the other marks that time, weather, and loving use leave behind.

Wabi originally stood for emotions that were sad, desolate and lonely, but poetically, it has come to mean things that are simple, un-materialistic, humble by choice, and in tune with nature. A phrase commonly used today in conjunction with *wabi* is 'the joy of the little monk in his wind-torn robe'. A *wabi* person epitomizes Zen, which is to say, such a person is content with very little; free from greed, indolence and anger, and understands the wisdom of rocks and grasshoppers.

Sabi, as said earlier, by itself means 'the bloom of time'. It signifies a natural progression – a discoloration, some hoariness, maybe some rust, the extinguished gloss of that which once sparkled. It's the understanding that beauty is fleeting. The word's meaning has changed over time, from its ancient definition of 'to be desolate' to the more neutral 'to grow old' gracefully.

The welcoming of imperfection into your life is at the heart of the Japanese concept of *wabi-sabi*, which, in a larger aesthetic context, means 'impermanent, imperfect and incomplete'. The word comes, as explained above, from two separate words. *Wabi* describes the creation of perfect beauty through the inclusion of just the right kind of imperfection, such as an asymmetry in a handmade ceramic bowl (contrasted with the precision of a machine-made bowl). *Sabi* reflects the kind of beauty that develops with age, such as that which occurs with the oxidation of a bronze statue.

Wabi-Sabi prizes authenticity. The cracks in an old teacup are viewed as assets rather than flaws. It is the true acceptance of finding beauty in things as they are. It is a way of life that appreciates and accepts complexity, while concurrently valuing simplicity.

Some say that *wabi-sabi* may have its roots in the Buddhist teaching of the 'three marks of existence' (*sanbouin*): impermanence (*shogyou mujou*), quietness (*nehanjakujou*) and the absence of self-nature (*shohoumuga*). In essence, life is about three simple realities: nothing lasts, nothing is finished, and nothing is perfect.

There is a whole tribe of *wabi-sabi* design enthusiasts (called 'wabibitos') today who abhor shabby chic. For them *wabi-sabi* décor inspires minimalism that focuses on the people who live in the space more than anything else. Possessions and other items are trimmed down to the essentials based on utility, beauty, or nostalgia (or all three). The colour palette sways towards whites and earth tones thanks to the use of natural materials. The approach is basically to live modestly, and learn to be satisfied with life as it can be once the unnecessary is stripped away.

37

YUUGEN

Yuugen is said to mean a profound, mysterious sense of the beauty of the universe.

How you interpret the word depends on the context. In philosophical texts, *yuugen* meant 'dim', 'deep' or 'mysterious'. In the criticism of Japanese *waka* poetry, it was used to describe the subtle profundity of things that was only vaguely suggested in the poems. *Yuugen* is not an allusion to another world. It is about this world, this experience the here and now.

Aesthetic ideals in the country are influenced mostly by Japanese Buddhism. In the Buddhist tradition, all things are said to be either 'evolving from' or 'dissolving into' nothingness. This 'nothingness' is not an empty space. It is rather a space of potentiality. If the seas represent potential then each opportunity is like a wave arising from it and returning to it. There are no permanent waves. There are no perfect waves. At no point is a wave complete, even as it reaches its peak. Nature is as a dynamic whole, a one entity that is to be admired and appreciated.

The concepts of *fukinsei* (asymmetry, irregularity), *kanso* (simplicity), *koko* (basic, weathered), *shizen* (without pretence, natural), *datsuzoku* (unbounded by convention, free), *seijaku* (tranquillity, stillness) and *yuugen* (subtly profound grace, not obvious) are all interconnected. Each of these expressions are found in nature and exist as virtues of human character. Virtue, therefore, can be instilled through an appreciation of, and practice in, the arts. Aesthetic ideals have an ethical connotation and pervade much of Japanese thinking.

Yuugen is most eloquently described in the words of Daisetsu Teitaro Suzuki, 'Yuugen is a compound word, each part, yuu and gen, meaning 'cloudy impenetrability', and the combination meaning 'obscurity', 'unknowability', 'mystery', 'beyond intellectual calculability', but not utter darkness'. An object so designated is not subject to dialectical analysis or to a clear-cut definition. It is something we feel within ourselves, and yet it is an object about which we can talk, it is an object of mutual communication only among those who have the feeling of it.'

All of this may sound very profound and philosophical, but for the Japanese, this is an intrinsic part of daily living and everyday life.

III

CULTURE

38

DERU KUI WA UTARERU

Deru kui wa utareru literally means 'the nail (stake) that stands up, gets hit/hammered down'.

Japan is a country bound by conformity and group thinking. In Japanese culture, therefore, anyone who is too different, too self-opinionated or too outspoken is viewed as a selfish show-off and a potential threat to the rest of the group. This is neither appreciated, nor liked.

Here, there is huge respect for the concept of harmony. Every effort is made to avoid conflict. Each individual tries proactively to not stand out, but to blend in. Consensus always comes first.

The interesting thing, however, is that Japan is also a highly competitive society. People strive to outperform each other in all spheres. High-school students compete like crazy to enter good universities. Workers single-mindedly focus on getting promoted.

And companies spend infinite amounts of money to outdo rivals with newer and better products.

So, how can competitiveness and consensus co-exist? Well, that is the inherent beauty of the Japanese culture.

The Japanese way encourages humility in the pursuit of excellence. So, it is not that traits like innovation and thinking out of the box are not recognized or rewarded, but in the Japanese system, there is no arrogance and, at most times, no public flourish for individual achievements. For one, most successes are attributed to team work. Two, success is celebrated together and an effort is made to carry every team member along.

Even at school, the accent is on attaining a balanced scorecard. If a student were to excel in one subject, the teacher would surely commend the effort; but, if the student were to lag in another subject, the teacher would worry about remedying the deficit more than feeling good about the good grades received. At work, too, just being good at your own trade does not guarantee growth within the organization. The ones who have special skills are respected and treated well, but they are not the ones who would generally be promoted to the next level. They have to be well-balanced in all aspects of the job, keep the harmony intact to gain promotions.

The interesting dimension to this maintaining of 'harmony' is that if a consumer electronics manufacturer, for example, invents a hit product, others follow with similar products, making the market highly competitive overnight. If a politician succeeds in building a highway in his constituency, other politicians would compete to do the same in theirs. The fight is always to attain common ground and overall parity. There is harmony and comfort in this parity.

There are good aspects to such healthy competition. It creates an even playing field, which leads to products being polished to state-of-the-art quality.

As elsewhere, Japanese companies too have been facing global competition, and as the nation's society changes, individual achievement is getting more and more recognition, but hostility towards the pile that sticks out is still there as a Japanese tendency in general.

The moral of the story is that the more original you are, the more you should keep yourself humble and grounded!

39

ENRYO

*E*nryo simply means 'restraining your speech/actions towards people'.

It is a sensitive Japanese concept. *Enryo* is integral in presenting Japan as a country, where people work to avoid conflict. *Enryo* could in everyday life mean not using your mobile phone on the train, or not throwing all of your trash in one big bag in a single go, or not lighting that cigarette wherever you want. At one level, simple acts of politeness; but actually, at a higher level, acts of self-restraint so as not to inconvenience others or create a situation that would annoy others. And to the Japanese, *enryo* sort of comes naturally.

In everyday language, *enryo* is often used to avoid an unpleasant linguistic phenomenon – the dreaded negative form. Basically the use of *nai*, which mean 'no'. So, rather than say *Tabako wo suwanaide kudasai*, which means 'Please don't smoke' and has a *nai* in *suwanaide*, it is much nicer to appeal to a higher civic sense with *Kitsuen wa goenryo kudasai*, which translates to 'Please refrain from smoking'.

There is another everyday dimension of *enryo* in Japanese etiquette. Suppose you are visiting a Japanese friend at her home. Naturally, it's polite for her to offer you tea or coffee. And polite for you to refuse. You should say, '*O-kamai-naku* (Please don't bother).' Of course, it would be polite for your friend to ignore what you just said and serve you the tea anyway. However, you should refuse several more times as she continues to urge you to join her in some more tea. Eventually, you are expected to give in and partake with a lot of hesitation. And you are supposed to only sip a little bit of tea. *Enryo!* All of this is the expected and accepted *enryo*. Similarly, say you are invited over to someone's house for dinner. Here, *enryo* becomes incredibly acute. Obviously, you are supposed to eat and drink, but not to exhibit too much *enryo*, as having nothing is also considered rude. Again, you must show reluctance, and lots of it. The hostess meanwhile has her own *enryo* to deal with. Although she has gone to great lengths to make a wonderful meal, and it's quite elegant, she will continue to repeat, 'You probably won't like this,' or 'This is all I could find in the house.' Pure *enryo*. The Japanese are really good at this self-effacing behaviour, and, as an outsider, it takes you a while to figure it out and comply.

There is another interpretation to *enryo*, which can be explained as 'examining things from a distance'. This is actually the application of an oft-used word, *Go-enryo-naku*, which roughly means 'Please don't be shy'. It is a constant invitation to open up and communicate, but, at a subliminal level, continues to keep a certain level of formality and decorum in every action and every interaction. In business, it remains an invisible barrier that cannot be crossed, irrespective of how close you are to the other person.

40

IKIGAI

❧

Ikigai is 'a reason to wake up each morning'. Also, 'the reason for being'.

It is very similar to the French 'raison d'être'. In Japan, the word is widely used to describe a healthy passion for something that makes one feel as though life is worth living to the fullest. *Ikigai* is often used to describe a devotion that one may have to something, to the extent that one may become quite obsessed or even consumed by it. It is common belief that everyone has an *ikigai*, although not everyone has fully comprehended, internalized or cultivated it.

Ikigai is often explained by Western thinkers through a Venn diagram with four overlapping qualities: what you love, what you are good at, what the world needs, and what you can be paid for. But for the Japanese, *ikigai* is above and beyond all this. The warrior-like energetic allegiance sets *ikigai* apart from any regular hobbies or interests. *Ikigai* makes one feel as though one is part of something special, which can be cherished and identified with as an inherent and inseparable part of oneself.

An *ikigai* is often described as an intense internal passion to carry out a personal mission that one may have a strong affinity to. One may not be able to reasonably explain why, but one may feel a magnetic attraction to explore a particular path and feel drawn towards anything that is associated with it. When one manifests whatever is pulling at their inner self, one receives an intense internal satisfaction, a holistic satisfaction in fact, which makes one feel fulfilled and gives new layers of meaning to one's life. The interest in one's *ikigai* can be so deep and strong that one may literally live and breathe it every day, and align to it one's mind, body and soul, even altruistically suffering for it if necessary. Regardless of the blood, sweat and tears that are shed to put in the work, one tends to stay loyal to one's *ikigai* and weather all storms that attempt to keep one away from it, once one has evoked and embraced it.

The Japanese say that finding and igniting their *ikigai* is not a complex task. When they are quiet and motionless, it is often the first thing that comes to their mind when they think about what they would do if they had as much time or resources as required to ignite it to life. The reason they mention 'life' is because an *ikigai* takes on its own energy, and once the creation has been birthed, it gains momentum so that it feels 'alive' to its creator.

Although an *ikigai* can be realized by pursuing a specific target or ambition or dream, it can also be something as simple as setting a goal for a new way of expressing oneself or interacting with others. For example, some people find happiness in just cooking for and caring for their family. Other people find joy in simple but meaningful acts of kindness towards others. This could also be unveiled by cultivating a mindset open to all new possibilities, so that one lets in a limitless amount of spontaneous and life-changing opportunities.

41

ISHIN DENSHIN

Ishin denshin is a Japanese idiom which denotes a special form of interpersonal communication through mutual understanding and without having to speak. It literally translates into 'what the mind thinks, the heart transmits'. Sometimes translated into English as 'telepathy', *ishin denshin* is also commonly rendered as implied as opposed to being said out loud.

Ishin denshin comes from Zen Buddhism. They say the ultimate enlightenment of Zen Buddhism can only be conveyed from master to disciple non-verbally after rigorous training.

Traditionally in Japan, men were not supposed to talk too much. Common aesthetics ingrained in them the idea that commitment is to be shown through action. Explanation was considered cumbersome and feminine, and was despised by men. 'Just do it' was their slogan, and it was manifest long before Nike made it its own.

Toshiro Mifune, the much-admired Japanese movie star who featured in many of Akira Kurosawa's movies, once featured in a TV commercial for a beer brand. All that the commercial had was a strong and silent Mifune and the message, 'Men drink Sapporo Beer, no words necessary.'

In Japanese movies too, especially the *yakuza* (gangster) movies, the leading character tends to be a quiet, intense man who doesn't even show his affection towards the heroine clearly, not to mention verbally. One of the typical lines in Japanese traditional theatre goes, 'Don't ask anything ... please understand.' No wonder the Japanese aren't too good at presenting themselves amongst the global crowd.

Thankfully, Japanese women don't share this 'aesthetic' urge to keep quiet. Or do they? In the old Japanese movies, beautiful heroines always seem to be quiet. For women or men, silence is golden. And the Japanese haven't changed a lot in recent years.

An interesting facet though is that if you have tried speaking to both Japanese men and women in English, you must have noticed that in most cases, women speak English better than men do. One cannot be sure if this is more of a cultural factor than just the matter of ability. Japanese men, at the bottom of their heart, don't seem to believe in explaining anything verbally, even in their mother tongue, to their compatriots, not to mention in English to foreigners. This must be the reason why more Japanese women are employed at the management level of global companies in the country, far higher than their employment levels in home companies, where they constitute no more than 9 per cent of the management cadre.

Non-verbal communication can be achieved only when you have a common homogeneous background. Some would say that the low female manager ratio in Japan is probably the result of male managers trying, maybe unconsciously, to keep the men's homogeneous world intact. This also explains why there are only a small number of expatriate employees in Japanese companies. Silence rules silently.

One interesting dimension to *ishin denshin* is that it is sincere, silent communication, via the heart or belly (that is, symbolically from the inside, *uchi*), distinct from overt communication via the face and mouth (the outside, *soto*), which is seen as being more susceptible to insincerities.

42

KAROUSHI

❧

Karoushi or *karoshi*, literally translated, is 'death due to overwork', death due to one's occupation.

While the West has been agonizing over 'work-life balance' for at least a couple of decades now, Japan has never achieved such a state of balance or living. What there is, instead, is a word for 'death by overwork'. It is result of Japan's notoriously gruelling work culture that has come under the scanner lately. Because every year, hundreds of Japanese people literally work themselves to death.

The medical causes of *karoushi* deaths are usually heart attacks and strokes due to stress, and possibly a diet bordering on starvation. This phenomenon is not the exclusive preserve of the Japanese. It is also widespread in South Korea, where it is referred to as *gwarosa*. In China, overwork-induced suicide is called *guolaosi*. But death at work due to overwork is more pronounced in Japan.

In recent months, the president of a Japanese ad agency, one of the largest in the world, had to resign from his position taking moral responsibility for the *karoushi* suicide of a female employee. The first case of *karoushi*, though, was reported in 1969, in a Japanese newspaper company where a twenty-nine-year-old worker died because of a stroke. The term *karoushi* was coined in 1978. A book followed in 1982, bringing the term into public discourse. In the late 1980s, several high-ranking business executives, who were still in their prime, suddenly began to die without any previous sign of illness, dragging *karoushi* deaths into the full glare of Japanese public life. So much so, that the Japanese ministry of labour began to publish statistics on *karoushi* starting 1987.

'Workaholism' in Japan has historically been driven by high work involvement, with most people compelled to work by inner pressures, and low enjoyment of work. For the ordinary Japanese salaryman, strenuous work hours get stretched further by overtime, and the addition of mandatory after-hours socializing and drinking that their job requires. Invitations to *nomikai*, or 'drinking parties' post work, cannot be turned down as these parties are mandated not for the employee to relax after a hard day's work but to build better connections between co-workers at the office.

An important side effect of *karoushi* is family depression in Japan. Men who become too busy with their jobs think less and less about their family. High levels of family depression exists as a result. The family, in fact, could be viewed as an obstacle to work.

The joke in Japan is that the suicide prevention hotline is often so busy that callers have to dial forty to fifty times before they can get an answer! Each year, roughly 20,000 to 30,000 people in Japan commit suicide (21,764 in 2016). A newly occurring phenomenon is a kind of camaraderie involved in the process of committing suicide, where people spend time searching online to find other suicidal individuals and then 'make plans to die together'!

43

KŌREIKASHAKAI

*K*oreikashakai is the phenomenon of an ageing society, a graying Japan.

The number of Japanese sixty-five years old or older has almost quadrupled, to 33 million in 2014 (in forty years), accounting for 26 per cent of Japan's population. In the same period, the number of children (aged fourteen and younger) decreased from 24.3 per cent of the population in 1975 to 12.8 per cent in 2014. The sales of adult diapers surpassed diapers for babies in 2014. This change in the demographic make-up of the Japanese society, referred to as population ageing (*koreikashakai*), has taken place in a shorter span of time in Japan than compared to any other country in the world.

The average life expectancy in Japan touched eighty-three in 2011. The median age, meanwhile, was 45.8, compared to just 26.7 in India!

According to projections, the current fertility rate will account for 40 per cent of the population by 2060, and the total population will fall by a third from 128 million in 2010 to 87 million in 2060. The Greater Tokyo Area is virtually the only locality in Japan to see population growth, mostly due to internal migration from other parts of the country. Between 2005 and 2010, thirty-six of Japan's forty-seven prefectures shrank by as much as 5 per cent, and many rural and suburban areas are struggling with an epidemic of abandoned homes (8 million across Japan).

All civilizations have always prayed for longevity of life. So why is Japan not celebrating its boon of long life? Well, there are a lot of concerns.

Social security spending, namely pension, medical care and welfare combined, is ballooning out of control. Annual government spending on these measures has increased 2.32 times from 1990 and crossed 110 trillion Yen in 2012. Coupled with the declining birth rates, the proportion of the population in the older age groups is actually scary. In current Japan, this means that the younger generation must increasingly bear more burden of social security.

More and more elders are suffering from dementia, but there isn't enough supply of caretakers and caretaking facilities. Elders in their nineties, suffering from dementia and other illnesses are being taken care of by their sons and daughters in their sixties and seventies, who are beginning to need the care themselves.

While the retired elders are sucking up social security spending, the elders who are still working in their sixties and seventies are taking away the job opportunities of the young. The young, less in number in the first place, have even fewer jobs today as a result. So a small working population has to support a large elderly population.

Some say that the average life expectancy of the Japanese will surpass 100 by the end of the century. Probably by then, the rate of population over sixty-five will be around 50 per cent.

Longevity and perpetual youth have been the dream of mankind; but longevity without perpetual youth in Japan is surely proving to be a nightmare.

44

NITO WO OU MONO WA ITTO MO EZU

Nito wo ou mono wa itto mo ezu literally translates into 'one who chases after two rabbits won't catch either', or trying to do two things at once will make you fail in both.

This is no different from the English proverbs 'he who chases two hares will not catch even one' and 'a donkey between two haystacks always starves'.

Organizations in Japan place a lot of premium on loyalty and fidelity. The true import of *nito wo ou mono wa itto mo ezu* is actually relevant to being faithful to your boss. In a Japanese organization, once you are faithful to your boss as a young man, you'd better stick to being faithful to him all the way through, unless he retires or loses his clout in the organization. Long-lasting fidelity is something Japanese men have worshipped since the days of Samurai warriors. And so it stays even today.

Stories abound in corporate Japan about *nito wo ou mono wa itto mo ezu* situations. Once upon a time, for example, there was this young man in a company who was very faithful to one boss for more than ten years. This young man was capable at work, so his devotion was very much appreciated by his boss and he was treated with much affection. His future in the company seemed secure until he reached middle management. Then came a time when his boss was promoted to a higher position and someone else from another department replaced him. The new boss was said to be the company's rising star. The young man, being innocent, now extended his loyalties to the new boss all at once, and worked harder, with even more devotion, than he had under his former boss. He didn't know that the former boss and the new boss weren't necessarily getting along with each other.

After a couple of years, a major restructuring and personnel reshuffle took place in the company. As is common with such reshuffles, it was influenced by a lot of internal politics. The new boss was sent away to do a minor job. The old boss returned, now even more powerful in the new structure. But he was no longer inclined to the young man because he had shifted loyalties to the new boss, not caring for his old relationship with him. The result inevitably was that the young man's future went up in smoke because of these divided loyalties. Such is the potential damage due to *nito wo ou mono wa itto mo ezu*.

The Japanese corporate environment is very unforgiving and it is not easy to navigate your way through the complicated maze of internal politics and intrigue. Most young people, who get caught in making a literal choice between the two rabbits (bosses) generally have a hard time. The future of young professionals has in the past decades been tied to the fluctuating fortunes of their immediate superiors. This is changing somewhat, but it will still take a long time in Japan for meritocracy to become the only yardstick for professional advancement.

45

OMAWARI SAN

Omawari San means a policeman. But the word carries a lot of respect and politeness in Japanese society. Its literal translation would be more like 'Mr Patrol'.

Japan is said to be one of the safest countries in the world. This may not be entirely true as news headlines there, like elsewhere in the world, still scream daily crime. But it is true that Japan is much safer as a country than most other parts of the world. Young women walk around city streets alone at night, never fearing assault, molestation or harassment; you never hear of a bank ATM being robbed, and the bag you left in a taxi will most likely come back safe to you.

You could attribute this safety to a variety of reasons. Low tolerance for drugs is surely one of them. Strict gun control is another. And, of course, a lot of the credit must go to the *Omawari San*.

Japan has a unique police system called *kouban*. Literally, this means 'rotation watch', and it stands for the small police huts you see everywhere in the nation's cities.

The prototype of this system was established in 1874. In the beginning, it was a small box meant for a one-man standing watch in rotation. Then, in 1881, it was transformed into local community stations with as many as six officers in each hut. Since then, it has been further systematized, and today the *kouban* is spread out nationwide.

Today, typically two or three policemen are stationed in a *kouban,* while others patrol the streets. Their official role is to enforce law among citizens, but, in reality, it appears they are busy giving directions to lost tourists, and taking care of lost items. They are friendly advisors to passers-by with problems. If someone finds a lost child, they will take the child to the *kouban* nearby. If someone is looking for a good sushi bar in the neighbourhood, they will go to the *kouban* and ask the *Omawari San*. Stories abound, like that of a man who lost his wallet and not only reported the incident, so the wallet could be restored to him in case it was found, but also asked the *Omawari San* to lend him some money. And, not surprisingly, the *Omawari San* did lend him the money!

The *Omawari San* has become a familiar figure in local communities. He performs important roles in all kinds of Japanese movies and comics. In fact, one of the most popular comic characters in recent times was an *Omawari San* called *Ryotsuin* in the *Kochikame* series by Osamu Akimoto. The series started in a weekly comic magazine in 1976, and lasted until 2016. The series became so popular that it was turned into TV animation, and then into theatre animation and even into a live action movie. The comic earned a Guinness Book of World Records recognition for 'The Most Volumes Published For A Single Manga Series'. The *Omawari*

San was a major character in the entire series and to date has fond recall value amongst the Japanese.

46

TATEMAE-HONNE

*H*onne and *tatemae* describe the contrast between a person's actual feelings and true desires (*hon'ne*, 'true sound') as opposed to the public behaviour and opinions (*tatemae*, 'built in front').

Tatemae and *honne* are two fascinating dimensions of dealing with the Japanese.

Tatemae, though literally meaning 'façade', is actually more appropriately 'face'.

Honne is 'honest voice': that inner voice of conscience.

Tatemae and *honne* together constitute in many ways the yin and yang of Japanese interaction, and negotiations. If you do business with Japan, you will be privy to both the public face as well as the true inner voice of Japanese business. It is not that the Japanese are hypocrites: that they say something else and mean something else. It is just that the Japanese do not always deem transparency as the ultimate virtue in a discussion. What you know, what you think and what you publicly say at most times may have many degrees of variance.

A 'white lie', the not-quite-true fabrication, or shading of the truth, that is designed to soften what would otherwise be a hurtful comment or uncomfortable social reality, is often resorted to by Western cultures. So, the Japanese behaviour is not really unique or peculiar to the country.

Tatemae is driven primarily by the Japanese notion that nothing in life, or business, is really black or white. The shades of grey in between, the ambiguity, is accepted as natural. It is not that the Japanese intend to be either deceptive or deceitful, but they do not always place all their cards on the table.

Some of this may also have to do with conveying bad news. The Japanese side, sometimes knowing fully well that it has no intention to go ahead with a deal, will politely nod, mistakenly communicating to the other side that the discussion is still in play. Actually, it is not a wholly bad tactic. It allows the Japanese to play along, stay engaged, and still have the leeway to eventually say no.

Easier to hide, than to negate.

The ways in which *tatemae* and *honne* can be juxtaposed is virtually limitless in Japan. *Tatemae* can be a way of maintaining modesty, highly valued in Japan compared to Western cultures. It can even be a way of maintaining position. Or it could just be a way of defusing an awkward situation. Or a way of flattering an important client.

An astute personal and professional antenna is what you require to deal with *tatemae* situations. Much of it is really a sixth sense you develop over time. You need to, for example, read into long silences. Or those agenda items that keep dropping down in the serial order. Sure signals that the Japanese are trying to wish away a troublesome matter.

There is an axiom in Japanese: *uso mo hoben, or* 'lying is also a means to an end'. It sums up the general attitude in Japan of tolerance of – even justification for – not telling the truth. This may take a while getting used to, but in Japan you quickly learn to live with it.

47

UCHI-SOTO

Uchi-Soto in the Japanese language is the distinction between in-groups (*Uchi*, 'inside') and out-groups (*Soto*, 'outside'). This distinction between groups is a fundamental part of Japanese social custom and is directly reflected in the use of the Japanese language itself.

The basic concept revolves around dividing an individual's outreach into 'in-groups' and 'out-groups'. When speaking with someone from an out-group, the latter must be honoured, and the former humbled. That is achieved with special features of the Japanese language, which conjugates verbs based on both tension and politeness. It may also include social concepts such as gift giving or serving. The *Uchi-Soto* relationship can lead to someone making great personal sacrifices to honour a visitor or other person in an out-group.

One of the complexities of the *Uchi-Soto* relationship lies in the fact that groups are not static; they may overlap and change over time and the situation. *Uchi-Soto* groups may be conceptualized as a series of overlapping circles. One's position within the group, and relative to other groups, depends on the context, situation, and time of life. For example, a person usually has a family, a job, and other groups or organizations to which they belong. Their position within the various groups, and in relation to other groups, changes according to circumstances at a given moment.

The workplace is a typical example: employees below a middle manager are in his in-group and may be spoken to using casual speech. His bosses or even, in large companies, people in other departments, are in an out-group, and must be spoken to politely. However, when dealing with someone from another company, the middle manager's entire company is the in-group, and the other company is the out-group. Thus, it is acceptable for the middle manager to speak about his own company, even his bosses, using a non-honorific speech. That emphasizes that his company is one group, and although the group may have subdivisions inside itself, it does not include the other company.

For example, when speaking with subordinates, a manager might omit the honorific *-san*, but he would be unlikely to do so when addressing his superiors. On the other hand, when dealing with an outsider, essentially any person not directly connected to his company, he omits all honorifics to speak about anyone in the company, including his superiors. However, when the same manager speaks to a subordinate about the subordinate's family, he refers to the subordinate's family, which is the subordinate's in-group but not his, in polite terms. However, he refers to his own family, which is his in-group but not the subordinate's, in plain language. Thus, the manager and the subordinate both refer to their own families as *kazoku* (family) and to the other's family as *go-kazoku* (honourable family).

In addition to features of the Japanese language, *Uchi-Soto* also extends to social actions. For instance, in a Japanese home the most senior family member, usually the father or grandfather, normally takes a bath first; the rest of the family follows in order of seniority. A visitor to the home, however, is offered the first bath. Similarly, an overnight guest is offered the best sleeping arrangements even if it greatly inconveniences the rest of the family.

48

YOROSHIKU

Yoroshiku is actually a derivative of the more polite word *yoroshii*, which stands for any one of or all of 'good', 'okay', 'fine', or 'well'.

Actually, *yoroshiku onegaishimasu* is the magic phrase that softens requests, expresses gratitude, opens doors and makes everybody feel good. Fundamentally the simplest, quickest and easiest way to understand *yoroshiku onegaishimasu*, and the less formal *dozo yoroshiku*, is to appreciate that it expresses both 'please' and 'thank you'. It is used to both make a request and to thank the person, before and after the favour is done. *Yoroshiku* is merely the casual version that gets used among friends.

Yoroshiku onegaishimasu is also most times used in place of *hajimemashite* when first meeting someone. What it basically means is 'Please treat me kindly' or 'Place me in your good favour'.

You can use *yoroshiku onegaishimasu* for so many things! If someone says it to you, most of the time protocol requires that you just say it back to them (matching their bow); unless they are clearly asking a favour, to which you can simply reply 'I understand' or 'Not at all'. It is important to know that, as an expression of humility, it makes the interaction more amiable, eliciting good feelings all around. It's an exquisite shorthand remark that conveys your acceptance of the indebtedness of all relationships.

The important point towards understanding this phrase is that it is not said with regard to something that has already happened, but rather an expression of gratefulness, regret, explanation, or another expression about a possible occurrence in the future. Its important function is to say *arigatou* (thank you) or *gomen nasai* (sorry) about something that has not yet happened.

In the use of this phrase, there are different levels of formality one needs to pay attention to. *Yoroshiku* is very informal, used with underlings and good friends. *Douzo yoroshiku* is less informal, used with colleagues. *Yoroshiku onegai shimasu* is more formal, used for someone higher up or when you are in doubt of which level of the expression to use. *Yoroshiku onegai itashimasu* is very formal and humble, used with clients and important people. Finally, *yoroshiku moushi agemasu* is exceedingly formal and humble, sometimes used in New Year's greeting cards.

This phrase is all about inherent humility. Even before any act of kindness or goodness is done, extreme courtesy has been shown by extending both appreciation as well as gratitude. This is what differentiates the Japanese culture from the cultures of the rest of the world. It is the sheer mindset that nothing in life is an obligation and that a willingness to engage in itself is an act that begets a thank you from the other person.

The Japanese have also evolved courtesy to different levels of finesse. As explained above, the degree of formality in communication is driven by not just how formal or informal the discussion is, but also by who is talking to whom. And in that, the hierarchy and the pecking order is well defined. So is tone and tonality. And civility. And humility. So much for nuance.

IV

FOOD

49

B-KYUU GURUME

B-kyuu gurume actually translates to 'B-class gourmet'.

B-kyuu gurume is a term the Japanese started to use in the 1980s, when it was first coined as a cynical reaction to the snobbish high-cost, high-class Japanese gourmet that had become much celebrated and famed over the previous few years, but remained well beyond the reach of the ordinary person. *B-kyu gurume* came to refer to common, yet rich everyday Japanese dishes that were the 'hearty-homey cuisine' of ordinary folk. It is important to note that although *gurume* is the Japanese version of 'gourmet', it doesn't mean a person who enjoys food; it refers to a type of cuisine. Many books have since been published, and many magazine articles have featured restaurants and joints where foods that can be labelled as *B-kyuu gurume* are available.

So what constitutes *B-kyuu gurume*? No simple answers here. But everyday favourites like *yakisoba* (fried noodles), *omuraisu* (omelette rice), *oyakodon* (chicken and egg bowl) and *udon* (thick noodles) are among the evergreens that come to mind immediately.

Add to that the two most favourite dishes of the Japanese populace today. Surprise! Surprise! Curry rice and Chinese soup noodles.

Curry had been brought to Japan by the British more than a century ago. So the Japanese didn't consider it to be an Indian dish. And, in the century gone by, the dish has evolved within Japan in its own unique way. The curry sauce stewed with meat and vegetables and poured on top of the rice is very very far from anything Indian, and does not even have a remote resemblance to the original Indian version. It is purely Japanese in taste and in appearance. Today, you can find dedicated curry rice chains everywhere in Japan, and it's a very popular menu item in restaurants and cafes too. With the help of packaged curry blocks and pre-cooked curry sauce sold at supermarkets, it's also one of the most frequently served dishes at home. Children love it. It's easy to cook. It is healthy. It is tasty. It is inexpensive. It has all the reasons for mothers to want to serve it often. So curry rice is No. 1 on the *B-kyuu gurume* list of favourites.

Unlike the curry above, it is not clear how the Chinese soup noodle or 'raamen' (more often spelled 'ramen') came to Japan. This everyday-everywhere favourite consists of Chinese-style noodles served in a chicken- and/or fish-based broth with various toppings on top. The dish has evolved in Japan for more than a century now. And, much like curry rice, is today sold and served everywhere in Japan. Mothers too love it. It's easy to cook. It is healthy. It is tasty. Making it a universal family favourite. Plus, it a close No. 2 on the *B-kyuu gurume* list.

B-kyuu gurume is food that best reflects the epicurean soul of the local populace. It is comfort food. It is everyday cuisine, popular with the masses. *B-kyu gurume* is best found in small *izakaya* (pubs) and restaurants. Reasonably priced and hearty, this *B-kyuu gurume* is tucked away in small eateries that exist in the shadows of the mighty skyscrapers of Tokyo. Inconspicuous and faceless, but temples of good, wholesome food.

The easiest way to find the best places for *B-kyuu gurume*? Just look for the places with queues stretching outside. You will know where the locals eat.

50

BOTORU-KIIPU

Botoru-kiipu simply means 'bottle-keep'.

It is a common practice among senior Japanese businessmen to buy bottles of liquor and keep them in the care of their favourite bar. The way this works is that a new bottle is bought and handed over to the bartender, who labels the bottle with the name of the patron. Every peg ordered and consumed is poured out of that bottle, visit after visit. So the liquor bottle basically remains in the safe custody of the bar but is the property of the patron, who has the right to partake of its contents over ensuing days and months. The bar merely charges a pouring fee per peg. And the bottle remains labelled and ready for its owner's use always.

The *botoru-kiipu* is a very visible signal of success, of having 'arrived', in Japanese business circles. The 'bottle-keep' basically announces status. It is like a membership to an elite bar. The right to keep and retrieve your bottle elevates you to a special status as an honoured guest.

To be invited out for a drinking session to one of these elite bars is very special. And a privilege reserved for only a few. The *botoru-kiipu* is fascinating not just for the simplicity of the thought of a 'mine-only' bottle, but also for the not-so-subtle signal it sends. An affluent host in Japan may actually have not just one bottle of liquor at a discreet and classy bar at Roppongi but possibly an entire mini-bar at his disposal! So, you would have a bartender literally wheel out an entire selection for you. You would notice that besides being neatly labelled with the host's name, the bottle also would have a neck-tag that would allow the bartender to keep track of how many pegs were poured, and when. All so very well organized!

The *botoru-kiipu* is a preserve of the top echelons of Japanese business. It is not driven by any sense of economy; that is, that drinks bought by the bottle would be cheaper than when bought by the peg. That may also be true, but the bottle held in trust by the bar is like being a member of a select inner circle. A place where you are recognized and well regarded. A place where they know you. A place where they take good care of you.

The culture of *botoru-kiipu* dates back to the end of the Second World War. That was the time when it was important in Japanese business to acquire a 'face'. Over the past fifty or sixty years, this custom has not really died down. It has just become more sophisticated. As a foreigner, being taken to the host's special bar is an honour. So evolved is the system that top customers even have bartenders more or less permanently assigned for them. If your host is really senior and special, then his favourite bartender could even be collecting champagne corks from all his parties and displaying them at your table in a special bowl, much like mini trophies of war!

51

DEMAE

❧

Demae is the Japanese word for 'home-delivery'.

For Japanese wives inundated with unexpected guests or businessmen working overtime at the office, everything from a steaming hot bowl of noodles to an entire meal is only as far away as the nearest telephone. *Demae* is a free doorstep delivery-service offered by many inexpensive neighborhood restaurants, and is one of the many charming amenities of Japanese city life. Though the Japanese may take it for granted, *demae* comes as a pleasant surprise to visiting foreigners, since such services have all but disappeared in their own countries.

The practice of *demae,* or food delivery service, dates back to the Edo period (long before modernization). Sushi, soba noodles, bento boxes (the most famous Japanese delicacies to this day) all originated in the Edo period and were available through home-delivery. Ever since, *demae* has gradually grown and expanded with the development of technology. First, telephones, then faxes, and finally the internet and smartphones. Perhaps drones will soon take over the delivery services. Who knows? The *demae mochi* (delivery persons), weaving their way through bumper-to-bumper traffic on their bikes with heavy trays or *bento* boxes are a common sight at lunch and dinner times in any city in Japan.

The *demae* ecosystem has expanded with time, and has gotten more and more sophisticated and responsive. It is not only the national food chains but even small restaurants that can today be accessed on the internet and a *demae* arranged. Each small restaurant may not have its own *demae mochi*, but today that facility is extended to these smaller eateries by dedicated food delivery websites on the internet that accept orders for their list of registered restaurants. Some restaurants are in fact outsourcing the delivery function itself. *Yoshinoya* (a famous global restaurant chain of beef bowls) started their home-delivery service in Japan through the national newspaper delivery system, which obviously was not active during the daytime and the evening.

Uber Eats, like in other countries, is today a further advanced food delivery business model. They specialize in delivering food from fine restaurants; they accept orders through smartphones; one of the registered drivers goes to the restaurant, orders the food, and then brings it to you.

Then there are internet services which deliver a kit of fresh ingredients for the dish you choose from the menu. All you need to do is to follow the instructions attached to the kit and the dish will be ready in ten minutes. You can order for any number of people according to your requirements.

People were surprised when Sharp, the famous electronics manufacturer, started similar food kit delivery services to promote their new state-of-the-art microwave series. Their menu was prepared by celebrity chefs and all the ingredients just needed to be put together according to the instructions and cooked in the microwave. A superb gourmet dish would be in front of you in just a matter of minutes!

Demae thrives in modern Japan. But the favourites do not seem to change: sushi, pizza and ramen remain the comfort food for hungry Japanese, wherever, whenever.

52

HARA GA HETTEWA IKUSA WA DEKINU

Hara ga hettewa ikusa wa dekinu simply means 'you cannot fight a battle on an empty stomach'. There is a lot of focus on food in Japan. The Japanese love their traditional fare. But some of it is changing.

Eating habits of the average Japanese have been changing quite rapidly since the Second World War. A typical Japanese breakfast fifty years ago was *gohan* (boiled rice), *misoshiru* (bean paste soup), *nattou* (fermented beans), *oshinko* (pickles), *yakinori* (toasted seaweed), *yakizakana* (broiled fish), *namatamago* (raw egg), *tofu* (bean curd), clams and some radish. Today, there is very little time to put together such an elaborate menu every morning. In fact, now, the number of people who partake in a Western-style breakfast with bread, rolls, cereal and eggs far exceeds those who have a traditional breakfast with rice every day.

During the catching-up phase of the Japanese economy in the 1950s and 1960s, most companies set up inexpensive and convenient *shain shokudou*, or canteens, for employees within their office buildings. With increasing options to choose from all around, and with a higher propensity to spend, *shain shokudou* in recent years were looked upon as the last resort for lunch – to be used only if you do not have enough time to go out, or if you do not have enough money to spend. But now, *shain shokudou* are back. They are upgrading their quality and starting to compete with restaurants outside. The good ones are well publicized and have started to attract outsiders. Nowadays, you can even find *shain shokudou* rankings on the internet!

In the case of Tanita Corporation, a manufacturer of digital scales, the recipe book of their health conscious *shain shokudou* has become a national bestseller, and sold close to 5 million copies.

But it is the bento, or more often adding a prefix of politeness, obento, that is the time-honoured treasure of the Japanese food culture. The most basic, simple, primitive, traditional and symbolic prototype of an obento is the *hinomaru*. It's just boiled white rice squeezed into an obento box with a red pickled plum on top. It's called *hinomaru* obento, or rising-sun box lunch, because the red plum in the middle of white rice resembles the Japanese national flag. But, actually, nobody takes the *hinomaru* obento seriously any more. There is an enormous choice of ingenious obento you could buy at convenience stores, supermarkets, department stores, privately run obento shops, obento shop chains, and carts on the streets.

The favourite genre of obento among the Japanese is probably the *ekiben*, or railroad station box lunch. From time immemorial, these were the original obento sold at each station of long-distance express lines, reflecting local cuisine, in order to serve the passengers on board. Now, the *ekiben* are becoming so popular that their distribution is expanding to highway rest areas, department stores and even the internet. In fact, it is fashionable now for famous department stores to hold *ekiben* fairs bringing different kinds of *ekiben* from all over Japan under their roof. Such fairs always attract enormous crowds.

53

ITADAKIMASU

*I*tadakimasu is very similar to saying grace before starting a meal. Generation after generation of Japanese have been taught to say 'Itadakimasu!' before partaking of the *oishii* food served in front of them. *Itadakimasu* can be translated into 'I humbly receive'. Children learn the expression from a very young age at home and no one can even think of starting a meal before others have received their share. This is taught as basic table manners to kids. At nursery schools, kids even sing an *obento no uta* (obento song) together and say *itadakimasu*. It's considered bad manners to start without waiting for everyone to have food before them and saying *itadakimasu*.

Somehow, roughly translated as 'Let's eat!' in the Western culture, *itadakimasu* has its origin rooted in ancient Japanese history. *Itadaki* is 'top' and is often used to refer to the top of a mountain. When ancient Japanese people ate food, they presented it to God as a humble offering, or when they received something from someone who had a higher position, they would first hold it above their head to show their appreciation and respect. From this custom, the verb *itadaku* is used as the *kenjogo* (one of the formal forms to show modesty) of *taberu* (eat) and *morau* (receive). And later, *itadakimasu* stayed on as table manners. The expression, in a way, therefore, relates to the traditional way of showing gratitude by elevating the gift (of food) received above one's head.

Saying *itadakimasu* has two meanings. One is to appreciate all the people who were involved in the preparation of the meal. The person who served you the meal, who grew the vegetables, who fished, and, of course, who cooked for you. The other meaning is to appreciate the ingredients. Japanese people always believe that even vegetables and fruits have a life, as do the meat and the fish. By saying *itadakimasu,* they show appreciation, as if saying, 'I receive your life and it becomes my life.'

The practice of *itadakimasu nohi* is actually the appreciation of nature, life, work, knowledge, and the people around you.

In Japan, there's a saying that seven gods live in one grain of rice. This emphasizes the idea that each morsel of food is precious. The heart of the *itadakimasu* ritual is one of sincere gratitude and introspection, even if only for a fleeting moment. In this context, commencing a meal with *itadakimasu* implies you'll finish all that is on your plate. Something gave up its life for the meal, so it is disrespectful to leave food behind on the plate.

Performing *itadakimasu* before a meal is simple and involves four steps: put your hands together; say '*itadakimasu*'; bow slightly; pick up your chopsticks and start eating.

Itadakimasu goes beyond the dinner table, into the everyday lives of the Japanese. It is essentially an expression of gratitude. Whatever you receive, be it a book, a job, or a ride to work, receive it with appreciation. Because, at its core, *itadakumasu* is a thankfulness for the things you've been given and a determination to make the most of what you have.

54

MIZU SHOBAI

izu shobai literally means 'water business'.

But it is actually a polite euphemism for the thriving nightlife business of bars, nightclubs, karaoke bars, geisha bars, cabarets, hot spring spas and all of the pleasurable businesses that lubricate the evenings of good corporate life in Japan.

Mizu refers to the soft, soothing and refreshing pleasure of water, which then dries off or vapourizes, perhaps more so, as it leaves no trace behind of the happenings of the night. *Shobai* is 'business', which is far more crucial and meaningful than the formal business of daytime. And distinct from *fuzoku* – the sex industry composed of soaplands, pink salons and image clubs.

Mizu shobai is central to Japanese business life because it is only when they are drinking do the Japanese actually let their hair down and not let hierarchical relationships of seniority or subordination come in the way of an evening of celebration and revelry. At the *uchiage,* or the 'job-closing party', it is actually a teetotaler who is looked upon with suspicion as he would perhaps be the only one the next morning who would be sober enough to remember the happenings of the previous evening. Which is really not a nice thing to do as Japanese office colleagues sing, laugh, gossip, deride, mock and make up over repeated rounds of *sake,* Suntory beer and Nikka whisky. And, oh boy, the Japanese can really drink!

Pretty young women can enhance the pleasure of *mizu shobai* as fraternizing with colleagues and clients in the evenings is a very well-established form of business etiquette in Japan. That it is also considered a corporate expense makes it even more legitimate and official.

One thing is for sure. And that is the infinite capacity of the Japanese to drink, drink, and drink. Also, most times, the ability to hold that drink. The Japanese can drown themselves literally to their gills till late at night, and then be as good as new the next morning, with no signs of a hangover from the previous evening. Visiting foreigners are best advised not to try to compete with their Japanese friends in drinking bouts. German or Punjabi, no one has much of a chance against them. The Japanese are pros at drinking. They have the capacity, and they have the daily practice! The Japanese can perhaps out-guzzle any other race on earth!

If you were to visit the nightlife areas of Shinjuku, Roppongi and Shibuya, you would also be exposed to the concept of *yukitsuke no ba,* which roughly translates into 'my favorite bar'. Every office group invariably has their favourite watering hole. In these bars, the group would be welcomed with special favours and showered with special service. The group and the group leader are accorded special status.

Mizu shobai, it was said twenty years ago, was fading out in Japan. It really didn't. Today, the 'water business' remains as liquid and as pleasurable, with no signs of any changing times that may dim the fun and frolic of corporate night outs. And remember, the return home requires a certain *ameo* for domestic peace!

55

MOTTAINAI

Mottainai is a combination of *mottai*, which indicates an air of importance or sanctity, and *nai*, meaning a lack of something.

Mottainai becomes a part of your Japanese vocabulary when eating with colleagues and associates. They polish off every single grain of rice in their bowl. Because, as children, they have been warned not to leave a single grain of rice in their bowls at the dinner table – such wastefulness would have been *mottainai!* The habit of eating all the food on one's plate is not only about discouraging waste but also about appreciating the efforts of the chain of events and people who made it possible to have food on one's plate.

Mottainai, therefore, conveys a sense of being sorry and concerned about waste. The expression *mottainai* is a combination of surprise and regret when something useful, such as food or time, is wasted. Quite like 'What a waste!' or 'Don't waste!' Besides

171

conveying 'wastefulness', the word is also used to mean 'impious' or 'irreverent', and 'more than one deserves'.

In ancient Japanese culture, *mottainai* had various meanings. Prime amongst these was a sense of gratitude, mixed with embarrassment, for receiving greater favour from a superior being than properly merited by one's own station in life. Buddhists traditionally used the term to indicate angst at the waste or misuse of anything sacred or highly valued, such as religious relics or spiritual learning. Today, the word is widely used in everyday life to indicate the wanton waste of any material object, time, or other resource.

The three Rs, reduce, reuse and recycle, convey the holistic meaning for *mottainai*. For those truly in tune with waste minimization, there is a fourth 'R': respect. Respect not just for the environment, but for the intrinsic goodness and value of everything, big or small. The respect dimension also stems from the Shinto belief that all objects have souls (possibly those of one's own ancestors) and therefore should not be discarded.

In fact, the Kenyan environmentalist Prof. Wangari Maathai showed off a T-shirt with '*mottainai*' printed on it at a United Nations session as a slogan for environmental protection. Her spirited championing of the effective use of limited resources – the spirit of *mottainai* – won Maathai the Nobel Peace Prize in 2004, making her the first African woman to win the prestigious award. Maathai's popular use of *mottainai* has made the word a part of the world's lexicon on environment and waste management. Waste not, want not. A very practical and down-to-earth approach.

For decades following the Second World War, Japan was a poor country. People recycled everything and wasted nothing. In Japan, even old *kimonos* are repurposed into beautiful accessories such as *nuno zori*, or cloth sandals, made from scraps of cloth and cord. *Kimono* cloth is recycled and reused in many other ways, including making purses, chopstick holders, glass holders and fans. You can even buy a set of chopstick rests made with *kimono* fabric imbedded in acrylic as a gift. Nothing and absolutely nothing is wasted. *Mottainai* is a state of mind and the booming Japanese prosperity in recent years has not changed the people's mind-set.

56

OCHA

❧

Ocha simply means 'tea'.

But it specifically refers to Japanese tea, which is by default Japanese green tea. Since *sencha* is the most common type of green tea in Japan, *ocha* generally refers to *sencha*.

Nowadays in Japan, there are infinite kinds of beverages to choose from. Besides the innumerable brands of beverages in pet bottles sold at convenience stores and supermarkets, many cafés and vending machines serve beverages on street corners too. But if you ask what is Japan's favourite beverage of all time, the answer is green tea. Among all kinds of pet bottled beverages sold today, green tea is by far the best-est seller!

It is believed that, like many other things, tea came to Japan from China. The history of tea in Japan can be tracked down to even before the Nara period (710–794 AD), when it was imported at the time of the Tang dynasty in China. But the history of tea as we know it today, started around the thirteenth century, imported along with Zen Buddhism, this time from the Sung dynasty of China.

The Japanese tea ceremony is well-known worldwide today. The tea imported from China spread among the ruling class: namely, aristocrats and warriors. And in the fifteenth century, under the reign of Shogun Yoshimasa Ashikaga (1436–1490 AD), the prototype of the tea ceremony was established by a Zen monk, Jukou Murata. In the sixteenth century, the genius Sen No Rikyuu (1522–1591 AD) appeared and brushed the style to today's perfection.

In the Edo period, the habit of consuming tea trickled down to the rest of the people too. Today, in most Japanese homes and offices you visit, the first thing you are served is a cup of tea. Many Japanese restaurants serve green tea for free while you are checking the menu. You shouldn't be surprised if a coffee shop offers you a free cup of green tea after you have finished a cup of coffee! Such is the ubiquity of *ocha*.

When a Japanese acquaintance asks you, '*Ocha ikanai?*' or 'Don't you want to go have some tea?', the meaning is not to be taken literally but that you are being invited for a conversation at a café. In this context, *ocha* means not only green tea but coffee, black tea or whatever you prefer to have at the café. Since Japanese homes and offices tend to be small due to the high prices of real estate, you find businessmen discussing business, couples gazing at each other lovingly, students studying, jobless ramblers resting, leisured housewives killing time at a café. It serves as an outsourced guestroom of the Japanese household.

There are many varieties of *ocha* available in Japan. Besides the ever-favourite *sencha*, *gyokuro* is the most precious and highly revered of the regularly served Japanese teas. Young buds, that too of only the finest and oldest tea plants, are cultivated with care and expertise. The result is a rare and expensive brew, sipped in tiny quantities, one sip at a time. You can also choose from a large selection of *bancha, honcha, genmai cha, mugicha, matcha, kobucha* and *kocha*. Cheers!

57

SAKE

❧

*S*ake, as most of us would know, is 'liquor'.

Sake in Japanese stands for 'liquor', also pronounced *shu*, and can refer to any alcoholic drink. In English, 'sake' is usually a reference to *nihonshu*, or 'Japanese liquor', and invariably just means rice wine. Under Japanese liquor laws, *sake* is labelled with the word *seishu* ('clear liquor'), a synonym less commonly used in conversation. In Japan, *sake* is the national beverage. It is often served with great ceremony – gently warmed in a small earthenware or porcelain bottles or flasks called a *tokkuri*, and then sipped from a small porcelain cup called a *sakazuki* (also *choko*).

In order to ask for *sake* in Japan, you need to call it '*nihonsyu*' or 'Japanese *sake*'. You may be asked at a restaurant, *Osake* (remember the prefix 'o' of politeness?) *wa nani ni nasaimasuka?*, or 'What do you want for a *sake*?' Then he (or she) is asking you to choose from beer, wine, whisky, *sake,* or whatever other alcoholic beverages there are on the menu.

There are, of course, many types of *sake* to choose from. There is *amazake,* a traditional sweet, low-alcoholic Japanese drink made from fermented rice. There is *doburoku,* the classic home-brew style of *sake.* Then there is *jizake,* a locally brewed *sake,* the equivalent of micro-brewed beer. *Kuroshu* is *sake* made from unpolished rice. And then there are specialities like *Teiseihaku-shu,* a *sake* with a characteristic flavour of the rice itself.

In Japan, *sake* is served chilled (*reishu*), at room temperature (*joon* or *hiya*), or heated (*atsukan*), depending on the preference of the drinker, the quality of the *sake,* and the season. Typically, hot *sake* is a winter drink, and high-grade *sake* is not drunk hot, because the flavours and aromas would then be lost. This masking of flavour is the reason that low-quality and old *sake* is often served hot.

Sake is traditionally drunk from small cups called *choko* or *o-choko,* and is poured into the *choko* from ceramic flasks called *tokkuri.* Another traditional cup type is the *masu,* where the box is usually made of *hinoki* or *sugi,* originally used in olden days to measure rice. The *masu* cup is crafted to hold exactly 180 ml (6.3 imp fl oz; 6.1 US fl oz). And, as tradition goes, the *sake* is served by topping the *masu* to the brim. There are *sakazuki* cups too shaped almost like saucers. These are favourites at weddings and other ceremonial occasions, especially at the start of the year or at the commencement of a *kaiseki* meal.

Sake is an intrinsic part of Shinto purification rituals. *Sakes* served to gods as offerings prior to drinking are called *o-miki* or *miki.* People drink *omiki* toasting the gods to solicit rich harvests in the coming year.

In a ceremony called *kagami biraki,* wooden casks of *sake* are broken open with mallets during every kind of Shinto celebration: traditional festivals, weddings, shop openings, sporting events, poll victories, and much more. This *sake*, called *iwai-zake* (celebration *sake*), is served freely amongst all to spread good fortune.

New Year's day is the occasion for the Japanese to drink a special *sake* called *toso*. *Toso* is a special variety of *iwai-zake*. It is traditionally made by soaking *tososan*, an old Chinese powder-like potion, overnight in *sake*. Even children sip some of this. In some regions, the first sips of *toso* are taken in order of ascending age, from the youngest to the oldest.

58

SHOUJIN RYOURI

Shojin ryori or *Shoujin ryouri* is the time-honoured dining style of Buddhist monks in Japan.

Shojin ryori grew in popularity with the spread of Zen Buddhism from the thirteenth century in Japan. As the meal is made without meat, fish or other animal products, it can be enjoyed by vegans, vegetarians and non-vegetarians alike.

A representative *shojin ryori* meal is served with soybean-based foods like *tofu* as the main ingredient. Seasonal vegetables and wild mountain plants are plated in the meal to bring the necessary balance and alignment to the body, mind, and spirit. This simple meal contributes to Japan's elegant haute cuisine called *kaiseki*, and can be eaten at the dining halls of famed Buddhist temples across Japan.

For vegetarians visiting Japan, finding the right food is always a challenge. If eating even eggs or fish stock is a no-no, then your choice of restaurants becomes really limited. In which case, a *shojin ryori* restaurant is your best bet.

Shojin ryori traces its origins in China. It used to be the food of the Chinese Buddhist monks. In the early thirteenth century, a Japanese priest, Dougen, went to study Zen in China. He brought back with him the concept of *shojin ryori*. Dougen's Zen sect, *Soutou Shu*, has ever since given the highest respect to the role of cooking the *shojin ryori* and the cuisine itself. So important is the cuisine to the sect that the priest who heads the kitchen is actually bestowed an executive position.

Shojin ryori interestingly uses 'the rule of five' in its cooking. Every meal therefore has to have five colours (green, yellow, red, black, and white), as well as five flavours (sweet, sour, salty, bitter, and umami), which are drawn out naturally from the ingredients, rather than added via additional flavourings. This balance between colours and flavours is believed to provide nutritional balance, while also bringing the body into balance with the seasons.

Shojin ryori developed unique recipes throughout its history in Japan, and has had a very big influence on Japanese food in general. For instance, it developed many recipes out of soybeans in order to supplement the protein that vegetarian food otherwise lacked. This resulted in the creation of soy sauce, *miso* paste, *tofu* (bean curd) and *natto* (fermented beans), to name just a few.

Another Japanese Zen sect, *Oubaku Shu*, created a parallel line of vegetarian cuisine called *fucha ryori*. This time it was the Chinese priests who brought the cuisine with them to Japan during the Edo period. So, this style of cuisine remained largely Chinese, but without impacting the popularity of *shojin ryori*.

Shojin ryori and *fucha ryouri* both exist all across Japan. It is just that *shojin ryori* restaurants are more numerous, hence a lot easier to find.

For those whose vegetarianism is not too strict, a *touhu ryori* (a Japanese noodle shop) or even an ordinary Japanese food restaurant can provide you with a good meal. But one must never forget that till the end of the Edo period (1868 AD), the Japanese were prohibited to eat any four-footed animal!

V

PHILOSOPHY OR WAY OF LIFE

59

AMAE

Amae is a Japanese trait that conflates concepts of 'dependence' and 'interdependence'.

It expresses a culturally ingrained dependence on authority figures and encompasses a wide spectrum of parent-child-like relationships.

Takeo Doi, a respected professor and psychoanalyst at the University of Japan, first referenced *amae* in his 1971 best selling book, *The Anatomy of Dependence (Amae No Kouzou)*. His inspiration to write the book came from the culture shock he experienced in the 1950s when he went to the US to study psychiatry. From this culture shock, Doi began his investigation into the Japanese psyche.

Doi sees *amae* as 'a request to be loved' – a universally accepted model of social behaviour in Japan. He says that *amae* is about living in harmony with others, and being able to depend on them just as a child depends on its parents and they continue to indulge the child even when it acts in a ridiculous or capricious manner. This sense of a close intimate relationship is one that Doi holds up to be an ideal in Japanese society, and one in which *amae* remains the secret ingredient. Doi explains that all babies are born craving love and closeness. They seek 'a sense of oneness' with their mothers through *amae* behaviours, acting helpless to encourage holding and cuddling. Traces of *amae* also colour adult relationships, such as when a woman or man playfully act child-like with a romantic partner to invite intimacy.

But the key application of *amae* is in the interesting interpretation of the Japanese idea of maturity, which is somewhat different from that of the non-Japanese. While the rest of the world thinks becoming mature is to grow into an independent, self-sufficient individual, the Japanese idea of maturity seems to be the realization that you continue to be dependent on others; that you are not living alone in this world, and this state can be positively exhibited in your relationships without inhibitions.

The open acceptance of *amae* or interdependence in human relationships is perhaps the reason why the Japanese are so good at joining forces as a team and working well together. And this has generally contributed positively to the overall development of the Japanese economy. The moral ideal buried deep in Japanese culture is to serve others before serving yourself.

At the same time, *amae* has been creating serious difficulties in the management of organizations. Take, for example, the Japanese value of unselfishness arising out of *amae*. The interdependent relationships encourage the Japanese to think of others first. This leads to problems in the decision-making process. At a department meeting, nobody wants to push through an idea. They would rather keep signalling each other with their eyes, implying 'you first'. In such circumstances, it is difficult to expect a strong leadership to emerge.

Whether one interprets *amae* as dependence or inter-dependence, it is deep-rooted in Japanese society. It may sometimes signal weakness, even indulgence, but as a society this helps the Japanese forge strong bonds of togetherness and trust. Bonds that endure, relationships that are secure, and a society that is held together by love.

60

FURIKOME SAGI

Furikome sagi literally translates into 'bank-transfer scam'. It goes back, in origin, to what are called *ore ore sagi* or the 'it's me scam'.

The *Yakuza*'s (gangster or fraudster) phone fraud conversation would go something like this:

The telephone rings. Old grandma answers.

'Hello?'

'Hey, it's me!'

'Yuzuru, is that you?'

'Yes! Grandma, I'm in real trouble. I just got into a terrible car accident!'

'Oh, no! Are you hurt? Is that why your voice sounds strange?'

'Yeah, that's why. Listen, Grandma, I had an accident with a really expensive car and don't have enough money to pay for the damages. Could you lend me some? If you don't, I might have to go to jail!'

'Of course, dear! I'll send you the money right away!'

Ore ore sagi is a scam where *yakuza* and other swindlers extort money from gullible victims by claiming to be a relative in dire straits. In the fast-ageing society of Japan, elders are routinely targeted. Major efforts have been made to warn the public, especially seniors, through media campaigns, about the scam, but despite the awareness created, the crimes continue unabated. It is reported that as much as 50 billion Yen is swindled each year by the ingenious and audacious *yakuza* through *furikome sagi,* which was officially so christened by the Japanese police in 2004.

Today, the fraud is becoming more and more deceptive. The entire scam is often played out by a group of people with one representing the victim's son or daughter, surrounded by side-characters such as their colleague, creditor or boss. In some cases, they don't even ask the victim to transfer the money, but ask for the cash to be brought to a certain spot. In other cases, the one who calls doesn't impersonate the victim's son but a lawyer representing him. There have been cases where the caller pretends to be a policeman. He asks the victim to cooperate in the sting operation to catch the culprit. As people get more cautious, the criminals keep inventing more and more elaborate traps.

Even though *furikome sagi* is getting more inventive, the target remains the growing elderly population. Old mothers, rather than fathers with a son; distress messages from a daughter living and working in a distant place, the script is largely the same. The cunning culprits don't take risks of hanging on to doubtful targets for too long. They keep calling until they hit a soft target, who seems to believe the caller is their child. Typically, old mothers living in the countryside are often lonely, looking for a chance to be of some help to others, hiding a substantial amount of savings of their own, and generally are very indulgent. And past data proves that it is not unusual for even younger persons to fall for this phone scam. And once you believe the identity of the person you are talking to, you tend not to doubt till the end.

And then, whenever a TV reporter interviews a victim, they always say, 'I thought I was cautious enough and would never be caught by such a cheap trick.' But somehow, everyone falls for the much-repeated *furikome sagi.*

61

FURUSATO NOZEI

The *furusato nozei* programme is a tax incentive scheme launched by the Japanese government to support the development of smaller, lesser-funded municipalities around the country. It is also referred to as the 'hometown tax' donation programme. Taxpayers can choose to donate to a city, prefecture, municipality or cause they want to support, such as the welfare of their hometown, or to social and environmental programmes in those locations, and aid distressed towns or cities in times of disaster. In return, a portion of the taxpayer's income and resident taxes are exempted, and moreover, they get to enjoy gifts of gratitude from the recipient towns and cities such as *wagyu*, melons, local *sake* and famous local goodies which are delivered to them.

Furusato nozei, or hometown, is therefore a programme that enables the Japanese taxpayers to shift a part of their tax money to any city of their choice. It was conceived by Yoshihide Suga, the then chief cabinet secretary, and introduced in the fiscal year 2008 to let people support their native towns in rural areas, supposedly in dire financial condition due to depopulation or natural disasters.

Technically, it's a donation to your city of choice. Most of this amount can be deducted from your next year's residence and income taxes. The amount of donation and deduction varies according to income, but in most cases, the maximum amount of donation has been seen to be about 30,000 Yen. A nominal one-time service fee of 2000 Yen is levied on the transaction.

Problems started when rural cities began to compete by offering alluring gifts in return for the donations. For example, Miyakonojou city of Miyazaki Prefecture, as one of several choice recipient cities, offers 500gm of quality beef, 300gm of sausages and 200gm of 'special sauce' for every 8,000 Yen of donations. So, if you donate 24,000 Yen, you get 1500gm of beef, 900gm of sausages and 600gm of 'sauce' for only 2000 Yen – the difference vis-à-vis the market price and after the service fee deduction. People have started to surf through the internet to seek such good bargains.

According to a survey conducted by the internal affairs ministry, prefectures and municipalities spent 63.3 billion Yen for these reward gifts in fiscal year 2015. That was 38 per cent of the entire donation amount. The total cost of such gifts amounted to 79.3 billion Yen, or 48 per cent of the donations received, if related expenses were included. This means municipalities ended up with only about half the donated amount for use.

In most cases, the gifts are local specialties. These helped promote local industries, which could further push the local economy, creating a virtuous circle. Unfortunately, competitive pressures pushed some cities to go as far as to offer IT gadgets, home appliances, precious metals, etc., and their websites almost looked like online shopping destinations!

It is said that the top twenty of those local municipalities collected 25 per cent of the nationwide total. The winners are those who offered popular gifts. Donors are using the programme as a way to get gifts worth a lot more than 2000 Yen for 2000 Yen.

Despite good intent, *furusato nozei* has become more commercialized than was initially intended, resulting in the actual 'hometowns' not receiving the support that they should have.

62

KUUKI

Kuuki means 'air'.

Much like the concept of *amae* or dependence in Takeo Doi's book *Amae no Kozo*, referred to elsewhere in this book, *kuuki* is a key concept that describes the uniqueness of Japanese culture. Shichihei Yamamoto's book *Kuuki No Kenkyuu*, or *A Study on Atmosphere*, published in 1977, became an instant bestseller. Books on 'Japanology' invariably sell well. However, this particular one on *kuuki* captured the public imagination like never before.

Kuuki's closest English translation would be 'atmosphere'. It's the prevalent 'mood', very similar to the Indian *hawa*. *Kuuki* is not initiated by any one person, it is not promoted by any one individual or set of individuals, but it just becomes the overall 'atmosphere' that influences the minds and actions of everyone around; so much so that it becomes almost politically incorrect to act contrary to the prevailing *kuuki*.

Yamamoto, in his book, picks up an episode of the battleship Yamato during the Pacific War as a good example of this *kuuki* at work.

Battleship *Yamato* was the largest and most equipped battleship of the Japanese Navy, and was worshiped as the symbol of the country's military power. However, when the Japanese Navy decided to send the battleship to the Battle of Okinawa, the purpose was not to win the war. By then, the Japanese Navy knew only too well that there was no hope for them to win. It was one of the notorious 'suicide attacks' and they knew it. *Yamato* and its crew were sent to Okinawa to symbolically fight until death (actually, 276 men survived out of 3332) in order to encourage the soldiers and the people of Okinawa to follow suit. Jisaburou Ozawa, lieutenant general of the Japanese Navy at the time, was quoted in a magazine article in 1975, thirty years after the war ended, saying, 'At the time, or even reflecting on it now, I think the suicide attack was the inevitable matter of course considering the overall *kuuki*'.

Take another example. The Trans-Pacific Partnership has been a thorny subject in Japan over the last few years. After the general elections of December 2012, however, the Liberal Democratic party won back the ruling position, and the new Prime Minister Shinzo Abe skilfully manoeuvered to create a *kuuki* favourable to joining the treaty using every opportunity, including some well-prepared *nemawashi* as well as his first visit to the United States to meet President Barack Obama. Once the *kuuki* was created, the opposition voices suddenly quietened down. The media blunted its criticism. People just started to say, 'You cannot help accepting it under such *kuuki*.'

In 2007, the term 'KY', which stands for *kuuki yomenai* or 'unable to read the air', became a buzzword in Japan and was even nominated for the annual Buzzword Award, a well-publicized award held every year since 1984 by a Japanese publisher. The word was used to mock the person who speaks or acts indifferent to the *kuuki* and, as a consequence, is treated as the oddball. Yet, there are enough people in Japan who would say, 'I would rather *kuuki yomanai* or "ignore the air" intentionally and become an oddball than just saying the words people want to hear.'

Obviously, you cannot win them all.

63

MAKERU GA KACHI

Makeru ga kachi literally translates into 'to lose is to win'.
A common English expression is to 'win the battle and lose the war'. *Makeru ga kachi* is actually the opposite of that. Sometimes, you can lose the battle and yet win the long-term war. If an immediate victory would be too costly or too difficult, then perhaps you should allow yourself a 'strategic withdrawal' – and focus on gaining an advantage in the longer term. That is the essence of 'to lose is to win'.

Makeru ga kachi contains a lot of practical wisdom in it. In the strictly hierarchical society of the Edo period, the people of the lower classes had no chance of winning a confrontation with the ones from the higher class. The ones at the top, the Samurai or the warriors, were actually allowed to kill anyone belonging to the lower classes on the spot for whatever reason. But in reality, the *Samurai* class was dependent on farmers, merchants and technicians in their everyday life. With the free market trade gradually growing, the non-*Samurai* class of people began to see a chance for success in each of their own trades. Only, they had to conform to the whims of whoever was above them, especially the *Samurai* class. They had to lose, or give in, in order to survive, and eventually win in the long term.

There are similar proverbs that abound.

Son shite toku tore, for example, means 'to bear a loss now to gain later'. It's a proverb of the merchant class, discussing the wisdom of their trade. The merchants of the time valued long-term customer relationships and it was their wisdom not to seek an instant profit but to acquire and retain a customer. Especially when dealing with the *Samurai* class.

Nagai mono niwa makarero similarly means 'let the long thing tie you up'. It's a proverb supposedly of the farmer class discussing the difficulty of challenging the rules imposed upon them. Here there is no 'winning' aspect any more. It's more like, 'to lose is to survive'. There were many farmer uprisings against heavy taxation imposed on them. Non-payment of dues invited severe punishments. To live and to survive meant that you at least lived to fight another day. If you were dead, there was nothing to look forward to.

In Japan, customer satisfaction and market share have always come before profitability. It is generally believed that once a pool of loyal customers has been built, profits will follow.

Manufacturers never seem to raise the price of their products, even if the costs start rising for reasons like the declining Yen rate. They are more afraid of losing customers than of losing money.

Makeru ga kachi as a time-honoured Japanese practice can actually find a place in global capitalism today.It is a concept akin to 'long-term management' contrasted to the Western obsession with 'quarterly results'. 'To lose is to win' highlights a long-term strategy that rewards patience and brand building over quick-fixes.

64

MOTENASHI

Motenashi, depending on how and where it is used, can mean 'manners', 'movement' or 'modesty'.

This is the simplistic interpretation of *motenashi* from the literature of the Heian period (794–1185 AD). If 'o', as a prefix character, is added to the word, it becomes *omotenashi*. These days *omotenashi* is used as a catchphrase to express 'hospitality', 'reception' or 'entertainment'. With the Tokyo 2020 Olympics rapidly approaching, the word *omotenashi* is being frequently used by the media to promote Japanese hospitality. The actual meaning of *omotenashi* goes way deeper than just referring to outstanding hospitality; the original meaning translates closer to 'entertain guests wholeheartedly'.

Among the virtues of the Japanese people, one thing every foreigner who has visited Japan will agree with is their warm hospitality. They are not only nice to you, but are always eager to help you in any possible way. Try and ask someone on a Japanese street for directions. If the person is not in the middle of something or not in a hurry, they will probably walk you to the place. Or, if it is a bit far away, they will probably draw you a map. Since foreign languages aren't a Japanese specialty(!), they will try to think of a way to somehow give you correct directions non-verbally.

The instant you step into a department store, female attendants will smile and bow to you. If you enter a café, the instant you take your seat, a waiter will come and place before you a glass of cold water and a wet towel. In front of some restaurants, you will find plastic replicas of the dishes served in a glass case, so that foreigners can know what to eat without having to decipher the menu. If you leave something behind in a restaurant, a waitress will surely run after you and return it. If you leave something in a taxi, all you have to do is take the receipt to the police station and tell the policeman what you have lost. He will track down the taxi for you in no time. There are small police stations on street corners all over Tokyo, where policemen are always waiting for the opportunity to help someone.

The key to Japanese hospitality is to anticipate what the guest wants in advance, and to offer the service before they can ask for it. Besides that, it is unwavering attention to detail, polite conversation, relaxed atmosphere and genuine smiles.

To the Japanese, hospitality comes naturally. It is something built into their DNA. Something from their time-honoured culture of 'you first'.

Make a Japanese friend and visit his home. He will keep offering you whatever is available, as well as keep on asking you if you are comfortable. And it is not even as if he is trying to be nice. He just cannot do otherwise. The meal will be elaborate. Much effort and love would have gone into its preparation. The service will be immaculate. Small touches like a flower in the vase not just to beautify the room, but to remind you of the season. Subtle. Never in the face. Such is the spirit of *motenashi*.

65

OJIGI

❧

Ojigi simply means to 'bow'.

It is well-known that the Japanese bow a lot. The expressions of greeting, gratitude, and apology are all accompanied by the gesture of bowing. The Japanese bow deeper to express gratitude, and deeper still to express an apology. The bow of greeting is practised both when you meet someone and take leave of them, as long as the other party is also Japanese. If it is a non-Japanese, they may prefer to shake your hand.

It is said that originally the gesture of bowing was to tell an opponent that there was no offence involved at all. By dipping one's eyes downward and submitting one's head to the opponent's mercy, one was virtually surrendering oneself, as if to say, 'I am all yours'. This explains how one gesture can convey three different types of messages, greeting, gratitude and apology, depending on the situation.

The older generation tends to bow deeper, longer and more often. If one were to go to the Japanese countryside, one would find old people bowing to each other as a form of greeting, over and over again. When one person ends his bow and raises his head, he may find the other one still bowing. So he bows again. If the other one ends his bow and raises his head, and finds the other one still bowing, he bows again! Funny, but an everyday occurrence for sure in Japan.

The bow of gratitude and the bow of apology can be witnessed easily on TV. The bow of gratitude can be seen when someone receives a prize or an award. Sometimes you might witness the receiver bowing and shaking hands with the presenter, at the same time. The recipient may also bow to the audience or to the camera with words of gratitude.

The bow of apology can be seen at press conferences of companies that have performed some kind of a misdeed. Multiple executives, standing side-by-side, bowing the bow of apology is a cliché of an image recurring eternally on Japanese TV.

In the case of an apology, if the usual bow is not enough to satisfy the opponents, there is an extra bow called *dogeza*. In this, the apologizer kneels down, hands and forehead touching the floor. Better still if the repentant apologizer would shed some tears and cry out 'I am so sorry' over and over again. This is the ultimate expression of apology. Well, if this is not enough, then there's no other effective way to apologize!

Many a time these exaggerated expressions of apology, even the *dogeza*, while visually very dramatic and moving, actually may not be as sincere as they seem on the surface. While deep regret is being expressed, in Japan, it would most times remain unclear as to why the misdeed actually happened and who actually is to be held responsible. So, there is apology and ritual bowing, but there is actually very little transparency. But then that is Japan. Sometimes, the ceremony is more important than the substance!

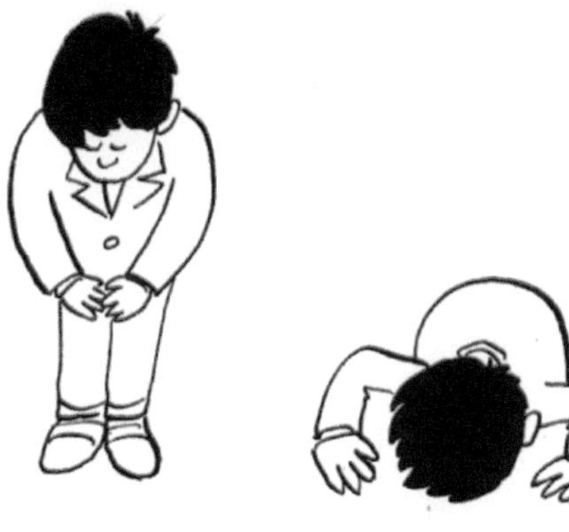

66

OMIYAGE

Deeply ingrained in their culture, *omiyage* is the Japanese custom of gifting.

It is considered very important in maintaining human relationships in Japan. An *omiyage* is a gift or souvenir carried back for family, friends and co-workers from a trip. But *omiyage* is so much more than just a souvenir. *Omiyage* is serious business. It can be a huge embarrassment for you if your co-workers come to know (easy these days from your Facebook, Twitter, etc.,) that you were out on a weekend trip, but returned to office on Monday without anything for them.

Omiyage is not discretionary. It is obligatory. It oils the cogs of Japanese society. If you go out of town visiting friends or acquaintances, you cannot return home (or rather, to the office) empty-handed. You just have to carry back some *omiyage* as a visible souvenir from the trip. A good *omiyage* makes a good impression all around. And makes for more cordial relations with friends and colleagues.

The most preferred and obvious *omiyage* choice is a local delicacy from wherever you have just returned. *Omiyage* boxes are usually bright and cheerful, containing individually wrapped snacks, which are perfect for sharing. They also vary, depending on the region. In Aomori, for example, the *omiyage* you would buy would all be apple-themed, while a short business trip to Hakone would require you to pick up a couple of boxes of *kamaboko* (pureed fish). Actually, almost every town strives to have a food specialty item of its own, commonly referred to as *meibutsu*, that becomes part of its unique identity. Therefore, if you are in Nagasaki, the specialty noodle, Nagasaki *champon,* is available everywhere and is easy to pick up and take home as *omiyage*. Similarly, the *kamameshi* sold at Nagano train station, a mixed rice dish served in traditional pottery, is a great *omiyage*.

Local foods or confectionery are preferred as *omiyage* as they are easy to pick, carry and distribute. However, when *omiyage* are being carried back for loved ones in the family, the choices would be more personal and tailored to perhaps a personal hobby or vocation.

The spirit behind *omiyage* has gotten somewhat diluted over the years. There is this general feeling that *omiyage* today is more about 'have to' than 'want to'.

Omiyage can sometimes be more weighty. Local lore has it that politicians and gangsters have been known to carry *omiyage* in confectionery boxes, but with cash hidden at the bottom of the box, when visiting an influential person to discuss difficult matters! Such bribery is not entirely unknown.

The Japanese 'you first' syndrome can also be observed in the terms used when an *omiyage* is presented to someone. The Japanese would say, '*Tsumaranai mono desuga*', or 'It's just something valueless', to show their humility. In Japan, it is considered bad taste to praise your own deeds. So, the humbleness. However, an American might well respond, 'Why are you giving it to me if you think it's valueless?'

67

ROUROU KAIGO

Rourou kaigo means 'old-to-old nursing'.

It is a rapidly emerging social problem in Japan. As more and more people get older, they need to be cared for. Infirmities can be both physical and mental. There is, however, a nationwide shortage of public nursing homes. So, the need for greater home care has spiked. But with the nuclearization of families there are hardly any young people at home available to help. Hence, 'old-to-old nursing'. The old taking care of the old. Not just that, tragically it could even be a more disabled person being cared for by a less disabled one.

Japan's ageing population is the highest in the world. And it is far ahead also in the speed at which the population is gaining in years. The ratio of those over sixty-five years in age against the total population was 26.6 per cent in 2015, while the world average was just 8.3 per cent. It is expected to grow to 29 per cent by 2020.

There are two obvious reasons for this alarming phenomenon. One is the growing longevity in Japan. The other is the declining birthrate.

Typically, in Japan today, ageing couples have no one else in the household to take care of them. If one gets sick, the other has no choice but to take care of them. But in this super-longevity society of Japan, even if they were to be living with their son or daughter, chances are that this offspring too could be over sixty-five years in age. It's not hard to find a ninety-something old parent being taken care of by their septuagenarian child.

On the other hand, healthy elders are livelier than ever before. They go to gyms and join athletic clubs. They jog. They travel. Their plan is to live an active life until the very last moment and die a death that minimizes suffering as far as possible. They also visit doctors ever so often and address any health issues as soon as they arise. All this further adds longevity to their lives.

On an average, one older person was supported by 2.4 persons in the working age bracket (twenty to sixty-four years of age) in 2012. By 2060, one in every 2.5 people in the Japanese population will be sixty-five years and over. One older person will be supported by 1.2 persons in this bracket by that year. The percentage of older people who lived with their children dropped from nearly 70 per cent in 1980 to 42.3 per cent in 2012. In contrast, the percentage of people aged sixty-five and over who live alone or with their spouse has only seen a rise. A 2012 survey shows that 'aged households' accounted for 21.3 per cent of all households. People aged seventy-five and over most likely live all alone. All of this is a big social concern in Japan.

The elderly who require nursing, and those taking care of them are both growing older together. There are no younger generations to take care of them. Japan's strict immigration policies also do not help. Care givers cannot be brought in from overseas. Public nursing homes are overstretched. Private ones are too expensive. Daycare centres are inadequate. The old have no choice but to lean on other old.

Rourou kaigo is a harsh reality Japan has to live with.

68

SAHOU

Sahou simply means 'protocol' or 'manners' or 'etiquette'. *Sahou* is the politically correct way to do things.

In Japan, if you want to participate in an event, you need to learn its protocol first. Whatever the event is, there are certain formalities to follow: rules for the set-up, priorities in the proceedings and who will do what, how and when.

Let's take a business meeting for example. Styles may differ from company to company, but whatever the case, the more important the meeting is, the more ritualistic it becomes. The papers are prepared according to precedent, participants are seated according to their order of rank, discussions proceed according to formal protocol and the decisions are made according to the *nemawashi* already diligently arrived at. It is extreme *sahou*. Everything is fixed in advance. And everything proceeds like clockwork.

Another good example could perhaps be a recruiting interview. First of all, your application documents need to meet the protocol requirements and should be in the prescribed form, sent attached with a covering letter, which again needs to meet certain long-standing norms. On the day of the interview, you need to wear a dark suit. When entering the interview room, you need to bow. Then turn around and shut the door while facing the door. Bow again and introduce yourself. Bow again and sit down. You have to be careful with your words when answering the interviewers' questions and not overstep conventional boundaries. The interview is highly structured and almost every step can be anticipated in advance. There is a lot of formality involved for both the interviewer and the interviewee.

It is not that you cannot do anything at the spur of the moment out of your free will, but it is important that you know the protocols and behave within the unwritten boundaries. It is like 'ad lib' in a jazz performance. Playing the wrong note will ruin the music. Sometimes brave innovators try to get rid of this stifling web of protocols, but don't seem to succeed in the long run. Fondness for ritual agenda is buried deep down in the Japanese DNA.

There is a governmental agency called *kunaicho* or the Imperial Household Agency, which takes care of the protocols of year-round ceremonial gatherings attended by the imperial family members. The Japanese imperial family not only attend the formal gatherings of dignitaries but very often visit the gatherings of common folks too. On those occasions, an army of preparation staff come in advance and lecture the protocol to the hosts and the attendees. Everyone needs to go through rehearsals more than once.

But relax. Nobody expects a foreigner to follow all the Japanese protocols. As a matter of fact, as long as you are visiting the places where foreigners often go, the ways to treat foreigners are well chalked out. You should play along and act as an ignorant *gaijin*.

Enough thought and preparation has already gone into welcoming you and in taking care of you. Enjoy it!

69

SHIKITARI

❦

Shikitari literally means 'social rules'.

This is actually very close to another Japanese word, *shuukan*, which translates into 'custom'. And very close in meaning is another word, *futsuu*, which simply stands for 'usual'. *Shikitari*, when used in conjunction with *shuukan* and *futsuu,* can therefore encompass the strictness of the social and traditional enforcement (sometimes rigidness) of the usual customs that make Japan what it is.

Shikitari gains major context in corporate Japan as the culture in most companies which kind of prescribes 'how we do things around this place'. This sameness of customs and rituals, also beliefs and behaviour, constitutes a major part of the norms that condition employees to work together as a team, in unison, and in complete harmony.

'Singing to a common hymn sheet' has been central to team work in Japan for many generations now. New team members kind of absorb the value system and the evaluation standards prevalent in the company through a slow diffusion that allows the imbibing of the culture of the organization. New recruits are, in a sense, soft indoctrinated by breathing in and living out a daily routine of do's and don'ts that define what is acceptable, and what is not. Much of this is actually achieved through active listening and observation.

Many of the *shikitari* signals are subliminal. The team members learn to work on cues that may sometimes look unintelligible to outsiders. But for those on the inside, the codification of customs, though never reduced to a rule book, is abundantly lucid and illuminating as regards the 'how to' on most tasks and projects. This in some ways also fosters a culture of mutual cooperation and mutual respect, such that disputes and disagreements too are resolved by mutual intervention, without much ado or fuss.

It is the *shikitari* spirit that is attributed to the phenomenal team work in Japanese companies. So strong is the herd mentality to conform that it is surprising that such teams are so open to change and innovation. May be this has something to do with the military drill-like coordination within the team, which helps them take on newer challenges together, knowing there is assurance and strength in working and prospering together.

In recent years, perhaps, some of the *shikitari* symbolism has started to weaken somewhat, especially in businesses that are more digital driven. There is slow change, but there is change for sure. Work places have become more casual, dressing for work has become more easy-going. Work timings are more open ended. There is even an easy informality which is non-hierarchical, with much less deference now placed on age and seniority. There is also more acceptance of individuality. So, the old order changeth, yielding to the new. *Shikitari* still remains the unshakeable foundation of older Japan, anchored in customs of yore, where teams remain bound by values and rituals they guard and perpetuate with missionary zeal. But at the same time, the new Japan, a younger Japan, is looking for more breathing space outside of monotonous conventions and customs, resulting in individual identity and independence.

70

SHINHATSUBAI

Shinhatsubai means 'newly launched' in the marketplace. A kind of fetish for the 'newest and latest'.

The term has continued to appear alongside 'new and newer' products as an advertising slogan providing unbelievable impetus for development to manufacturing industries, especially fashion. Every week, new products are launched in the Japanese market, most of which are destined to disappear within a few weeks. In this context, however, 'new' does not necessarily mean a novel product, newly invented, rather most times it is some bauble, device, gizmo, or added-value function that has been attached to a product that already exists in the market.

It is said that the Japanese fascination with 'new' products is like the *sakura*, the cherry blossom. It blooms for two weeks, and the Japanese get so very emotional while the *sakura* is out, but then it passes and the mood is gone. The Sakura Syndrome is one unique reason that the Japanese economy is constantly in an overdrive. This syndrome, because of its aesthetic and cultural underpinnings, has an irresistible charm. The Japanese become very excited about new fashions and ideas, but the trends only last a short while as then they get easily bored.

For years and years, post the Second World War, Japan got into a never-ending cycle of consumption. A cycle, best described as a relay of one 'boom' after another. There was the 'bowling boom' in the '60s; and in the '70s the 'Versailles boom', which took its name from a theme about the French Revolution in *Takarazuka* theatre (all-women opera) based on the popular comic series by Riyoko Ikeda. In the '80s came a spate of explosions: the 'ethnic food boom' with special interest on their Southeast Asian neighbours, the 'Italian boom' in food and clothes, the 'Shouken boom', the mindless grab for stocks as the market skyrocketed (the common joke being that even idle housewives were earning fortunes sitting at home), and the 'Onsen (Hot Springs) boom'. Then there was a 'Spanish boom' followed by the 'Tiramisu boom' with Italian desserts everywhere. The boom of booms was the 'Izanagi boom', the fifty-seven month non-stop growth of the economy in the '60s, which was challenged by the 'Heisei boom' growth since 1986.

Shinhatsubai is a potent concept. A kind of advertising madness that springs from the world of commercial consumerism. *Shinhatsubai* campaigns blanket the visual space of Tokyo with a peculiar kind of energy. In Tokyo's highly driven and high-energy market, *shinhatsubai* best expresses Tokyo's consumerist mindset. In other countries too, newness appeals and sells, but in Tokyo, newness seems to have become an obsession.

Shinhatsubai does more in Japan than merely oil the wheels of commerce. It provides a social distraction, and at the same time promotes a kind of social cohesion. It also contributes to and illustrates an ideology that defines cultural life. It governs means, modes, distribution, consumption and legitimacy. Thus, it provides 'meanings' – ideology constructs that define subjectivity. The Japanese hunger for fashion is almost barbarous, for it produces innovation without reason and imitation without benefit!

But *shinhatsubai*, at its heart, is simply the Japanese way of saying, 'change is good' in a land wedded to tradition and custom.

71

SHOGANAI

❧

Shoganai is all about accepting your fate in Japan. Translated into English, *shoganai* means 'it can't be helped'.

And, this expression is often used in Japanese culture, thinking and values. It is essentially a philosophy that says that if something is out of your control, it is better to quickly accept it and move on.

Shoganai explains how Japanese people can deal with terrible situations, such as disasters, without complaining. It also explains how Japan recovered so quickly from the Second World War, after many of its cities were completely destroyed.

Some argue that *shoganai* can have a negative effect too. For example, many Japanese people disagreed with the nation's actions during the Second World War, but didn't speak up. Extreme right-wing nationalist elements in the country seemed too powerful to fight, so it was *shoganai*.

In recent times, *shoganai* is often used to explain why many Japanese are unhappy with government policy, but don't bother to vote for a change.

The problem of *shoganai* is deeply ingrained into the very fibre of Japanese society. There is an understandable degree of *shoganai* toward being non-intrusive in matters concerning others, but the Japanese people allow their acceptance of a given situation to go far beyond just being considerate, to a point where it is most times self-degrading.

The society right now, in many ways, has created a tense atmosphere, where the expression of opinions contrary to what is popularly accepted views (in other words, the first expressed idea unconsciously absorbed and allowed to take precedence) is looked upon unfavourably. Even with the chance that a new opinion would be seen as more favourable than the presently existing view, the idea of *shoganai* suppresses the desire to allow that opinion to be expressed. One therefore fears being stigmatized if one expresses one's ideas independently and fearlessly.

The traffic is terrible. *Shoganai.* The meeting went unexpectedly bad. *Shoganai.* The client is being very unfair. *Shoganai.* The weather is too hot. *Shoganai.* The pragmatic attitude of *shoganai* helps save a densely populated island nation from going crazy due to stress and pressure.

Shoganai, or *shigata ga nai*, the more polite version of the word, is not just 'it can't be helped, so why worry about it?', but can also be interpreted as 'it is inevitable, so nothing can be done'. One can see this as a negative (just give up) attitude, but one can also see this as a proactive suggestion to avoid futile (and needless) effort.

There is this heart-warming story from eastern Japan just after the Tohoku earthquake in 2011. The entire area was facing a power shortage. Wherever possible, at home, in office and even in public spaces, electricity had been cut off wholly or selectively.

Escalators headed downwards in all public areas, including railway stations had been shut off. Most supermarkets had dimmed their lighting. The Japanese have seldom had to consciously conserve energy. But this was *shoganai* time. Nobody complained about the 'new hardship' that the earthquake had brought on. It was not even worth mentioning, just to be shrugged off and borne without a thought. So, the *shoganai* spirit is about going the extra mile without argument or anxiety or anguish.

72

TSUUKIN

Tsuukin means 'commuting to work'. And, if you say '*tsuukin* rush' it just means 'rush-hour commute'.

Commuting has always been a nuisance for the Japanese workforce in big cities, especially in the Tokyo metropolitan area.

Tokyo's population is said to be around 13 million, but it actually expands way beyond, because of its borders with the neighbouring prefectures. Prefectures like Kanagawa, Chiba and Saitama are seamlessly connected to Tokyo, and are actually an intrinsic part of Greater Tokyo. The population of Greater Tokyo area is around 35 million (depending on the definition of the area). The Tokyo-Yokohama area is the largest population cluster in the world concentrated in one area.

Thanks to the highly developed public transportation system in Japan, the nuisance of commuting is not caused by traffic jams, as in other parts of the world. The problems are due to the long distances, the lengthy travel time and the overcrowding. Since offices are concentrated in the central part of Tokyo, a large part of the commuting population flows in and out of Tokyo every morning and evening. And very late at night too. Because of the very expensive real estate prices, most citizens have their homes outside Tokyo where housing is more affordable. Spending one-and-a-half hours one way to get to work is the general norm, and no one seems unduly bothered by it.

Tokyo has its share of haves and have-nots. The haves are the ones who have their homes within a 30-minute commute from work. The have-nots are the ones who do not have a home in the centre of Tokyo, and, on an average, commute about ninety minutes each way. Assuming 250 work days every year (just for argument's sake, 365 days minus 104 weekend days minus eleven holidays), the have-nots spend an extra 500 hours a year in *tsuukin* alone. Surely that's punishing for the have-nots!

Commuting by the bullet train has become the preferred choice for those who can afford this more expensive mode of transportation. With bullet train lines spreading in all directions, one could be living in any of the historical resort areas around Tokyo and still commute to the centre of the city in relative comfort and in a much shorter time, making the *tsuukin* more bearable. But then not everyone can afford the bullet train to work.

The hellishly overcrowded regular trains and subways are what everyone lives by. It takes more than a certain amount of fortitude to survive the *tsuukin* on these everyday trains. The famous photo of Japanese railroad staff pushing a crowd of passengers into an already full train car has surely been seen by most of us. *Tsuukin* rush is unbelievable. There is just no space between one passenger and another; male or female notwithstanding. Everybody is just squashed together. Body squeezing against another body. Body pushed into another body. All becoming one massive tangle of human-kind. Everyone just stares into the ceiling, avoiding eye contact with anyone else, and yes, praying to god that no one farts!

73

UCHI NO KAISHA

Uchi no kaisha needs a little explaining. *Uchi* is more like a 'home', where someone belongs. *Uchi no* means 'our' or 'our family/ house' and *uchi no kaisha* means 'our company'.

Japanese men address the company they work for as *uchi no kaisha* or 'our company', as if they are talking about their family. This was more so in the past, when the seniority system and lifetime employment were intact, but still, until now, there are family-like sentiments attached to how the Japanese feel towards the company they work for. Many Japanese men still spend their whole career in one company: entering the company as fresh college graduates, and being there until their retirement age. So *uchi no kaisha* is actually a reality of their lives, an intrinsic part of themselves.

The women employees don't normally stay on that long, on an average, in a company. So, they seem to show a less family like sentiment towards their companies. But then the influence of women in corporate Japan is in any case somewhat limited. There are far fewer women than men in the workplace to begin with, and they largely conform to the overall norms in the company.

There are many fringe benefits attached to working in a Japanese company, large or small, maybe more so with large companies that support such a familial sentiment. Japanese companies seem to have a mutual-benefit system in place with these lifelong employees. In a manner of speaking, they live off the other.

The company invariably provides the employee (and most times, his immediate family) health insurance, medical support, low-interest loans, leisure support (corporate villas, sports facilities, discounted tourism, etc.), pension, and even honorary club memberships for the retired ones. Besides these, the company may provide the employee with some gift money at the time of a marriage, childbirth, and even death in the family. Many Japanese companies host their employees on overnight trips to hot springs, a cherry blossom picnic, a family field day, or something similar at least once or twice every year. Some of these perks and privileges may be disappearing now since Japanese capitalism does not support some of these soft touches any longer, but the broad concepts are very much alive in most companies even today.

Also, it is common that the companies support the employees' after-hours club activities in sports and hobbies, such as soccer teams, chess clubs, fishing clubs, or whatever. The business divisions they belong to often put together monthly fees every payday for a fund, which can be used for their holiday season parties, occasions of celebration, farewell and welcome parties, et al.

When you take into account all of the above, you can easily see how the company and the employee are so closely wedded; it is no wonder the employees of Japanese companies nurture a family-like sentiment toward their companies. The companies shower countless support and benefits; the employees reciprocate with undying loyalty for life.

And, of course, it doesn't end there. Most employees who retire from a company at the age of sixty, just go back to work again. They accept slashed wages to stay on, sometimes in a reduced capacity. But it is important for them to stay connected with *uchi no kaisha*. They know no other world, so to say.

74

UNTEN MENKYO JISYU HENNOU

Unten menkyo jisyu hennou is 'voluntary discontinuation of driver's licence'.

In Japan, fatal car accidents by elderly drivers are increasing. It's no surprise because the elderly population is continuously growing with the increase in life expectancy. Drivers in their eighties are not unusual in Japan. According to the national police agency, the percentage of drivers over the age of seventy-five causing fatal car accidents has increased from 7.4 per cent in 2005 to 12.8 per cent in 2015.

And there is frequent bad news on TV every day on this subject. One old woman crashed into a supermarket when she tried to park her car in front of the store and stepped on to the accelerator instead of the brake. One old man found himself driving against the traffic on a highway and collided head-on with a truck coming from the opposite direction, after he entered the highway from the exit ramp by mistake. Another old man ran into pedestrians after driving around for one whole day, but he couldn't remember where he was or how he got there.

Thus, a governmental initiative, a programme called *Unten menkyo jisyu hennou* or 'voluntary discontinuation of driver's licence' has been launched. The idea is to encourage elderly drivers to give up their driver's licence for their own good. Local municipalities offer incentives in exchange, such as coupons for bus, train, taxi and other transportation services, as well as discount coupons for hotels, restaurants and entertainment facilities. The police issue an ex-driver ID card to such 'renouncees' because the Japanese often use their driver's licence as their ID cards. The ex-driver ID card is a plastic card which looks just like a driver's licence and if you show it, you get extra services at shops that have identity stickers on their doors. So a lot of effort is being made to take some of the pain arising out of this voluntary giving up of the licence.

Consequentially, the number of voluntary licence discontinuations by the drivers over seventy has risen from 17,949 in 2006 to 2,31,233 in 2015.

The problem is actually with the elderly drivers living in rural districts. Depopulation has resulted in public transportation facilities becoming bankrupt in these rural areas. There are no other means of transportation except for automobiles. For elderly drivers living in such places, giving up their licences therefore has meant that they have no choice but to move into an elderly care facility as their mobility becomes zero.

Of course, there is also the view that taking away licences from the elders in rural Japan is really of no use, because these are remote areas where there is no one to be seen driving, or even walking, for miles and miles. So there is no real danger of these seventy-five or older drivers actually hitting anyone.

Meanwhile, in an interesting twist to *Unten menkyo jisyu hennou*, Emperor Akihito renewed his driver's licence in 2017 at eighty-two. But then, he only drives inside the palace. And he has reportedly said that this is going to be the last renewal of his licence!

75

YAKUSOKU

The simplest translation of *yakusoku* is 'promise'.

Traditionally, the Japanese as a society have tried to keep away from disputes and litigation. In the older days, and in the current times too, for that matter, a court of law is best avoided. This is not just because the legal process is expensive, but taking recourse to the law is seen as both uncivil and somewhat cowardly. Normatively, the society encourages a more peaceful orientation to the resolution of disputes and disagreements.

This understanding brings us to the concept of *yakusoku*. In the past, business in Japan was predicated on 'verbal agreements', which bound parties to an agreement based on principles of honour, goodwill and mutual commitment. Without being committed to paper and formally signed off, these agreements were sacrosanct.

Also important to understand is that the Japanese approach to writing legal documents is somewhat dissimilar to the West.

Lawyers in the western world tend to get very detailed in both the phrasing of clauses in a document, and in defining every contingent situation that may likely arise in the execution of the contract. The Japanese prefer to keep agreements more general, more open-ended, so as to allow more flexibility in the interpretation of what has been agreed upon. To outsiders, this can be somewhat disconcerting, but in the Japanese cultural and business context, the need to keep some leeway in the documentation is driven by an inherent trust that both sides need to show in the relationship. To understand this fully, you have to develop a deeper appreciation for the overall context of doing business together. The inherent premise is that when two parties agree to do business, there has to be mutual accommodation and mutual respect. Such mutual understanding cannot willy-nilly be created, cultivated or enforced by just the existence of a legal contract.

What is fascinating is the celebration that accompanies the signing of important deals. There is, of course, the drinking, but there is more importantly the *tejime*, the Japanese custom of ceremonial rhythmic clapping, typically accompanied by enthusiastic exclamations by the participants. *Tejime* is performed to signify the close of a bargain or other business negotiations signalling fulfilment, realization, and completion. The *tejime* begins with an '*ote wo haishaku*' call from the leader or the boss, after which the participants, just before clapping their hands, usually yell '*iyoo*' or '*moitcho*' in order to synchronize timing.

Tejime is an abbreviated form of *teuchi de shimeru*. *Teuchi* literally means 'clapping', but it also means 'to strike a deal' or 'to come to an agreement'. And, the word *shimeru* means 'to tie' or 'to fasten'.

The *tejime* spirit and the bonhomie has been the underlying foundation on which *yakusoku* has thrived over the years. A word of honour. Inviolable. Enforceable not by law, but by personal ethics and societal commitment.

And, by the way, for those curious about the clapping of hands, there are actually many types: the '*itch-jime*', which consists of a single clap, the '*ippon-jime*', which consists of three sets of three claps and one final clap (3–3–3–1), and finally the '*sanbon-jime*', which consists of three '*ippon-jimes*' (3–3–3–1, 3–3–3–1, 3–3–3–1). You have my word for it that every '*jime*' is uplifting and unifying for the team, and a reiteration of commitment to the contract!

76

YOKONARABI

The word *yokonarabi* can be broken up into two parts. *Yoko* refers to 'alongside each other', while *narabi* means 'in a line with'.

In English, this could translate as 'being in lockstep with', but colloquially it translates closer to 'keeping up with the Joneses'. In the context of corporate Japan, it is used to describe the frequent habit of companies doing things simply because their competitors are doing so. But it is really the Japanese commoner's habit of doing just exactly what his neighbour, his peer or his co-worker is doing that defines *yokonarabi*. Some critics prefer to call it 'horizontal assimilation'. Some sociologists just feel it is the fear of being left behind.

Yokonarabi can be witnessed in small nuances. Let us start with the workplace. Workers dress similarly to their peers. White shirts are near universal in Japanese offices. Even the young punks, the young IT geeks, the new movers and shakers in most companies tend to dress like each other. As if they have a common identity.

Yokonarabi extends again to something as simple as taking a vacation. As per company rules, any employee can take a vacation at any time, provided it is approved by his senior. But the problem is that a Japanese worker refuses to take a vacation when everyone else around him is working hard. He just feels guilty taking off when there is so much work to be done and everyone else is so busy. So what happens is that all the employees decide to take off at the same time, to avoid any guilt. Consequently, since everyone is on vacation at the same time, New Year's and Golden Week become chock-a-block with leaves. Everything is overcrowded and overfull. Everyone is headed to the same popular destinations at the same time. That is *yokonarabi* for you.

Yokonarabi abounds everywhere. Women buy the same Louis Vuitton bags. Kids buy the same games. *Yokonarabi* is driven by the common notion that you do something not because you yourself think it is good to do, but because you want to avoid the negative perception for not doing what others are doing.

Yokonarabi also explains the prevalence of fads that sweep Japan so often. Japan as a country always seems gripped by one fad or another. There is an expression that Japanese people become instantly hot and instantly cold, meaning they get excited about something very quickly and get bored of it just as fast. And it all happens to everyone at the same time. This is also a good thing sometimes, because such me-too consumerism has created a tidal wave of sorts, the Cool Japan culture of manga, anime, *otaku* and fashion that is uniquely Japanese.

So prevalent is this herd mentality, so to say, that there is an old joke you may have heard.

When the Titanic was about to sink, the captain decided to tell the male passengers to let children and ladies take the lifeboats first.

He said to the Englishmen, 'Act like a gentleman'.
He said to the Americans, 'Be a hero'.
He said to the Germans, 'It's the rule'.
He said to the Japanese, 'Others are doing the same'.

77

YUTORI SEDAI

Yutori sedai refers to the 'pressure-free generation' in Japan who received their primary and secondary education in the Japanese system during the late-1980s to the 2000s (the precise definition varies), when the standard curriculum shifted from an emphasis on soaking in knowledge and memorizing lessons to a new system that supposedly facilitated independent thinking and creativity.

During the 1980s, the Japanese government shifted its public education policy of primary, junior high and high school towards a somewhat relaxed curriculum. This was in response to the criticism that the public education system was putting too much pressure on students, and the overheated competition was distorting their personalities.

Starting 2002, the school week became five days a week from six; and the report cards became 'absolute evaluation based' rather than 'comparative evaluation based', to further reduce pressure. The students who underwent studies under this new curriculum policy are called *yutori sedai*, or the 'pressure-free generation'.

But this easing up did not last long. From 2009, school hours began to increase again. Also public opinion shifted back to encouraging the tightening up of the curriculum, since it was felt (not necessarily proved, though) that the average academic standards had fallen as a result of this policy and were consequently holding back the country's global competence. So, *yutori sedai* started somewhat to go into a rewind.

With this as a backdrop, *yutori sedai* as a phrase is most times used in a contemptuous manner, referring derisively to this entire generation of young people as somewhat half-baked and incompetent.

The *yutori sedai* started entering the Japanese corporate world from 2008, and this created its own set of problems. The widespread image of the *yutori sedai* in the Japanese media is that they tend to focus on their own self-realization and are completely indifferent to competition. In the vertical culture of corporate Japan, they are therefore seen to be strangers. HR departments have been forced to invent new ways to 'educate' them.

First of all, reprimanding them doesn't seem to have any positive effect. Two, they lack self-motivation. They don't initiate any move on their own until they are told what to do. They think it's their boss's job to set a strategy and give orders. They just follow the manual. They are very protective of their private time and would rather spend it with their personal friends than attend an office get-together in the evening.

But this may sound almost like a déjà-vu to an earlier generation of the Japanese that has been called *shin jinrui*, or 'new humans', in the 1980s, and was treated by the older generation as if they were strangers. Similarly, Japan has seen the 'bubble generation'. In the

1970s, those born after the Pacific War were labelled 'different' too. It happens perhaps, with every passing generation.

The fact is that as generations get younger, they just resemble younger generations in other parts of the world. That is the true impact of globalization. Japan cannot remain isolated for all times.

78

ZANGYOU

Zangyou is 'overtime' in Japanese. Combined with *karoshi* (death from overwork), these are the two major scourges of corporate Japan.

The Labour Standards Act of Japan stipulates that a worker's extra working hours, that is beyond forty hours per week, must be compensated through overtime. But one needs to understand the origins of *zangyou* from a very different perspective. The culture of over work and overtime unsurprisingly goes back to the end of the Second World War. With large parts of the country reduced to rubble by bombings, and two cities devastated by the nuclear holocaust, Japanese focused their zeal, energy and patriotism towards rebuilding the nation from ruins. Much of the economic miracle that followed was fueled by long working hours in the service of Japan. Driven by their intense loyalty to the country, Japan's corporate warriors persevered through endless hours of overtime, day after day, en route to a brighter future. In a mere thirty to forty years, Japan was able to transform itself into the economic power described in Ezra Vogel's famous work, *Japan as Number One*, through nothing but honest, hard work.

That all these long hours also got compensated through the payment of overtime, was a necessary corollary. And these earnings were not insignificant. A substantial part of the monthly salary of a Japanese executive was actually *zangyou* and materially contributed to the well-being of the family. In fact, it became a problem for Japanese executives when they were promoted to the management level, as no *zangyou* is paid to senior staff. As a result, pay packets would actually shrink. Many executives would honestly not have hesitated to give their promotion a pass, but this, of course, is not possible in the Japanese corporate culture. You had to accept the promotion in the interest of your long-term job security, even if that meant that a pay package without *zangyou* was much lighter.

But the times are changing. Lifetime employment itself is under threat. Managements of companies are under pressure to prune benefits like overtime as they make Japanese companies globally uncompetitive. Especially after the Financial Crisis of 2008, Japanese companies are trying hard to eliminate *zangyou* altogether. Many companies are allegedly forcing their employees to work extra hours without compensation. The government itself has started discussing the possible implementation of 'white collar exemption', a new set of laws that will allow more flexible employment conditions, namely fixed annual compensation without overtime.

Itochu Corporation, one of Japan's leading trading companies, experimentally implemented a new overtime scheme in October 2013. It banned all overtime work between 10pm and 5am, the time zone which was compensated by 50 per cent more than the usual overtime, and shifted it to 5am to 9am. The results have been mixed, with no firm conclusions to gain insights from.

To understand the true extent and impact of excessive and prolonged overtime, in one landmark case in 2014, a restaurant chain was found to be liable for the suicide of a manager, who had put in an average of 190 hours of overtime every month, that too for seven consecutive months prior to his death. During those seven months, he had barely taken two days off from work! But one cannot be sure that this act of *karoshi* was company-driven or compelled by the lure of *zangyou*.

VI

SOCIAL

79

BŌNENKAI

A bōnenkai is literally a 'forget the year gathering'.

Bōnenkais are Japanese drinking parties that take place at the end of the year, among groups of co-workers or friends. The purpose of the bōnenkai, as the name implies, is to forget the woes and troubles of the year gone by, and look to the new year with renewed hope. Of course, all of this partying is accompanied by the consumption of copious amounts of alcohol. A bōnenkai does not take place on any specific day; bōnenkai are dotted all through December.

Bōnenkai parties derive their origin from old Shinto religious beliefs dating back many centuries. The Shinto religion emphasizes purity to pave way for the upcoming new year. The intent perhaps was to get clean and pure by forgetting all the unpleasant things that occurred in the past year. So bōnenkai in the modern day context are 'year-forgetting' parties where friends, acquaintances, co-workers and even families gather just to have fun, and blank out all the pain of the past twelve months with a lot of drinking and dining.

Bōnenkai parties are held one after another, day after day, during December by each and every group that an individual may belong to, such as the company, division in the company, social organizations, business counterparts, relatives, friends and more. December is a tough season for the stomach. In fact, you see a lot of TV commercials for digestive medicines on air during this season!

Bōnenkai can come in different shapes and sizes. They can be formal or casual, or somewhere in between. Large ones are normally hosted in a hotel ballroom. Somewhat smaller ones are organized in a large restaurant, or in a large hall in the company premises. Smaller ones spill over to restaurants and bars in the city.

Since December is bōnenkai season, dining and drinking places all over Japan put in every effort to lure customers by offering special treats. On the other hand, the season is a nightmare for young employees who are chosen for the role of *kanji*. The person who is in charge of organizing the bōnenkai is called *kanji*, which means 'organizer'. Popular places get booked up well in advance. The people you are supposed to invite are busy attending other parties. Deciding on the time and venue is not easy. All of this requires planning well ahead of time.

More often than not, since it is the 'year-forgetting' party, the attendees are allowed to speak and act more freely than usual. In most cases, the most senior person around announces, 'It's a *bureikou!*' or the occasion where you can act freely regardless of rank and seniority. This means that subordinates can relax and have fun, relieved from the formalities of Japan's vertical society. Bōnenkai can therefore be a great opportunity for the young ones to become closer to their seniors. But you have to watch out and not go too far.

If you interpret your senior's *bureiko* announcement literally, you may end up regretting your behaviour for the rest of your career!

It is recommended here that you also read the piece on *kuuki* for connected insights.

80

CHUUGEN & SEIBO

Chuugen and *seibo* are seasonal gifts of gratitude sent to persons you are indebted to in some way or the other, especially prior to the country's two big autumn and winter holidays: before *obon* in August and before *oshougatsu* or the New Year.

Chuugen and *seibo* are usually called *ochuugen* and *oseibo* – the prefix 'o' added to express politeness. Both are long-respected features of Japanese life that can be traced back to the Edo period, or even further back. These gifts were originally delivered by hand, but are now mostly shipped by mail prior to the holidays; *ochuugen* before *obon*, or the Buddhist holiday welcoming the dead back home in August, and *oseibo* before *oshougatsu*, or the New Year's holidays. During these two big holidays, Japanese families get together in their hometowns where their parents and grandparents live, much as in Diwali or Christmas.

While *chuugen* and *seibo* continue to be widely practised, and are still popular in Japan, with the passage of time, observers say that the overall market for this kind of gifting has started to shrink. There can be multiple reasons for this.

The biggest reason probably is that the large business houses that used to send out gifts to a long list of clients have started to trim the list of recipients. Some companies have in fact completely quit the practice. The public reasons proffered are more moralistic and ethical, but in reality, it is actually cost-cutting, no less, no more. Some companies do genuinely feel that the habit of seasonal gift-sending has become old-fashioned and obsolete, an empty formality kept alive by inertia and needless custom. Such companies have started to curtail gifts to their clients, and also urge their employees to avoid sending gifts to each other.

Meanwhile, public servants at government offices have been banned from receiving such gifts, which could easily be mistaken as bribes. Teachers have started sending back gifts to their pupils' parents for the same reason. On top of that, since the Personal Information Protection Law came into effect in April 2005, obtaining people's home addresses has become very difficult. Given all these issues, the *kuuki* (the general atmosphere) is tilted towards discouraging the sending of *chuugen* and *seibo*.

While the old order changes, new realities are taking shape. The availability of e-commerce options on digital and mobile platforms have opened up a market for *puchi gifuto*, or 'petit gift', favourites with the younger generation of Japanese. Instead of limiting themselves to only two occasions in the year, the younger Japanese have started to send small gifts anytime they feel like it. These gifts are obviously not as expensive as the ones suited to company-to-company *chuugen* and *seibo*, but they surely have more meaning and emotion attached to them.

Gifting is in the DNA of the Japanese. You can't take that away from them. They just love sending and receiving gifts. So while the traditions of *chuugen* and *seibo* may be somewhat on the wane, the institution of gifting is well and alive. Also delinking the gifting to specific occasions has made it an anytime-anywhere-anyone phenomenon, and also helped remove the stigma of ulterior motives that can be attached to company gifts.

81

DANDORI

Dandori means 'arrangements'.

Dandori is all about the management of a programme, a process or a plan. And the Japanese are extremely good at this. It does not matter whether the planned event is small or big, in Japan, habitually, the whole thing needs to be documented, detailed and delivered with precision.

The *dandori* has its origins in the process management system of the *kabuki* theatre. Everything from the script, dialogues, set, positions of the actors, entry calls, cue sheets, lights, sound coordination ... every single detail was planned, thoroughly detailed out, and shared with everyone on the team, so the performance could be delivered to perfection, with the utmost coordination, and no surprises. The same rigour, the same planning, the same detailing is followed even today by Japanese teams whether they are implementing the staging of a big soccer match or a big commercial exhibition or, for that matter, a product launch. Work starts with the preparation of a thick implementation manual with the names and identities of all the staff members, their roles, and the timetable they have to follow, down to every detail that can be thought of, from the day they start the preparation to the day the implementation ends.

Even at a private party, a printed *shikishidai*, or a 'party timetable', is usually handed out to all the invitees at the door. It tells you clearly what is happening where, and when. The Japanese don't like to be surprised (no wonder, surprise parties are not popular).

This is why package tours appeal to the Japanese psyche and have always been money-spinners in Japan. Package tours run by operators detail out every little step of the trip. The itinerary is documented, the look-see-shoot stops are planned, the restaurants are reserved, the menu is pre-ordered, and the transport and hotels are well organized. But, most importantly, the tour guide keeps time for the entire group, ensuring that everything proceeds as per schedule and the entire group remains together. The Japanese find great comfort in all this 'packaging', such that everyone knows what to expect and there is no scope for any surprises. Package tours are, in a way, *dandori* in action.

The flip side of *dandori* is that the Japanese are good at planning, organizing and executing any event as long as there are no accidents. But once an accident occurs, the Japanese are perhaps not quite equipped to handle the situation. In the Japanese 'you-first' way of working, it can take hours to arrive at a decision. Elsewhere mostly, people are more accustomed to working to a command hierarchy, where everyone is clear on whom to look up to for directions and instructions in case of a crisis. In the Japanese system, anything that meanders outside the implementation manual automatically becomes a challenge.

Actually, it is okay for the Japanese to plan everything ahead in detail because in the country, everyone, absolutely every single person, is conditioned to delivering everything as planned on time. Elsewhere in the world, you cannot count on that. So, while planning works well for the Japanese, a little bit of flexibility and a margin for error are more the norms outside the island country.

82

GIRI NINJOU

G*iri* refers to the obligation one has to repay a favour taken. *Ninjou* refers to the sympathy one feels obliged to show to one's acquaintances.

Combined, *giri ninjou* means the moral obligation that you feel you need to fulfil in favour of the people you know. One who takes good care of his friends and acquaintances is described as *giri ninjou ni atsui*, or someone 'full of *giri ninjou*'.

No one really knows the actual origin of the concept, but *giri ninjou* is an old moral duty shared broadly amongst the Japanese. The fact that the concept is often used in traditional theatre as a dramaturgy informing a tragedy suggests that it could perhaps be traced back to the Edo period. *Giri ninjou* is still present in some modern-day movies and novels, especially in the ones depicting *yakuza*, or Japanese gangsters.

In most such dramas, a leading character who is 'full of *giri ninjou*' gets torn apart between *giri* and *ninjou*, because *giri* usually stands for the somewhat formal obligation towards the ones who have given you social support, while *ninjou* usually stands for a more private obligation towards a comrade or lover or someone you personally care for. It mostly happens that to fulfil one obligation, one has to betray the other.

A typical *yakuza* movie goes something like this. A boss of a gangster group gets killed by another group after a long struggle for power between both factions. The protagonist, a stranger who has been taken under the wings by the boss who was killed, feels obliged to take revenge. But the beautiful daughter of the boss stops him since revenge means either his death or an even more devastating counter-attack from the rival group. Nothing happens between the protagonist and the daughter, but there is a suggestion that they are attracted to one another. Complying with the heroine's urging, the protagonist tries to control himself and not take part in the conflict, but the struggle between the gangster groups goes on without him. However, after his group sees a major defeat in a fight, the protagonist can no longer desist and decides to go and kill the boss of the other group, leaving behind the beautiful heroine begging him not to go. In the climax the theme plays in the background, 'If you put *giri* on one side of a balance and *ninjou* on the other, *giri* weighs more in the man's world'.

Speaking of *giri*, one cannot but mention *girichoco*, or 'obligatory chocolate'.

It has become a custom for Japanese girls to present chocolates on Valentine's Day to the guys they like. And, over the years, it has become common for girls to give chocolates to all their close male acquaintances. Women at work are especially obliged to give chocolates to their bosses and colleagues. Thus, it has come to be called 'obligatory chocolate'.

In contrast, if it's really meant to show one's affection to the recipient, it's called *honmei choco*, or target-aimed chocolate!

83

GOORUDEN WIIKU

Besides the New Year's holidays and the Obon holidays, there is another major holiday every Japanese family looks forward to. It is called *Gooruden Wiiku,* or the 'Golden Week', which starts at the end of April.

Gooruden Wiiku is a set of important, individual national holidays concentrated in about a week: namely Showa Day to commemorate the Showa period under the reign of the late Emperor Hirohito (29 April is Emperor Hirohito's birthday), Constitution Memorial Day (3 May), Greenery Day (4 May) and Children's Day (5 May). Combined with the weekend, it becomes a longish non-working holiday.

The National Holiday Laws, promulgated in July 1948, officially declared nine holidays. Since many were concentrated in the week spanning the end of April and early May, many leisure-based industries experienced significant spikes in their revenues. So much so that in the year 1951, the film *Jiyū Gakkō* recorded the highest-ever ticket sales during this holiday-rich week, more than at any other time of the year (including New Year's and Obon), and set the ball rolling for the week's commercial significance. This even prompted the managing director of Daiei Film Co. to dub the week as the 'Golden Week' based on the Japanese radio lingo 'golden time', which denotes the period with the highest listenership ratings.

While New Year's and the Obon holidays are somewhat connected with ritual beliefs and people are tied up with traditions and family gatherings (although not as much as in the past), the Golden Week is mostly devoted to family travel and leisure. During the Golden Week, the Japanese often travel around the country, or abroad. This means that tourist attractions in Japan are overcrowded during this time. The same goes for airports and train stations. It is widely known that it's difficult to get reservations for accommodations and transportation during the Golden Week. For more and more Japanese, especially for those living in Tokyo, the new norm is 'staying nearer, spending more'. So shorter domestic trips or just staying on in Tokyo and enjoying the vacation is becoming equally acceptable. A visitor who was in Tokyo a few years ago during the Golden Week was struck by how, between the Tokyo Skytree, the world's tallest free-standing broadcasting tower, encountering its first Golden Week since opening in 2012 – Tokyo Disneyland and commemorating its thirtieth anniversary, and Tokyo Station, that was entirely renovated, it seemed like the whole of Japan had gathered around the Tokyo metropolitan area!

For foreigners visiting Japan during the Golden Week, there are both advantages and disadvantages. Weather in early May, springtime, is very pleasant and it is a good time to be in Japan. But the entire city is full and completely sold out. So, prices are really *takai,* or expensive. However, the hustle and bustle in Japan during

Golden Week is really enjoyable. Much to do, much to see, much to experience and much to spend on.

To make it all very authentic, if in Japan during the Golden Week, don't forget to hang a flag of a carp (a fish) for every member of the family. The carp hung on Children's Day during Golden Week, as per local legend, could become a lucky dragon!

84

GOUKON

❧

Goukun is a 'matchmaking party'.

The traditional 'arranged marriage' has become relatively unpopular and uncommon due to the Americanization of the lifestyle of the Japanese youth. Instead, *goukon*, or 'matchmaking parties', provide an opportunity for young people to find their partners.

Goukon initially started to enable college students to meet with the opposite sex. *Goukon* therefore traces its origin to the word *goudou compa*. *Goudou* means combined or merged. *Compa* is a code for parties, emanating from the word 'company'. In the pre-war period, *compa* were the drinking sessions held by male students who shared the same class, the same dormitory, or the same club activity. Men and women went to different schools back then. And, in the past, female students didn't consume any alcohol.

After the war, under the American influence, male and female students began to go to the same schools. There remained a few female-only schools, but even so, girls started to drink. That's when the prefix *goudou* appeared before *compa*. *Goudou compa* now started to mean parties with boy groups and girl groups coming together. It became a precious opportunity for shy Japanese youngsters to meet the opposite sex. The word was abbreviated to *goukon* later, when it wasn't only for students any more.

Actually, *goukon* is not always a matchmaking party. Many are just there for fun, with none of the members seriously seeking a partner. It is not unusual sometimes to find a married person at the *goukon*. But howsoever it may appear on the surface, all the attendees secretly expect a magical encounter to occur. This is because there aren't many other opportunities for them to meet someone outside their immediate circle of work and friends. Especially if the attendees are in their thirties, always busy at work until late in the evening, almost every day. Also, the Japanese are shy, and tend to go out with acquaintances in the same circle over and over again.

Generally speaking, *goukon* are intended not to result in a one-night stand, but rather for making friends and possibly forming a long-term relationship. Groups of men and women typically sit opposite each other, converse with one another, and share with each other what they find attractive for potential partners. Sometimes games are encouraged to reduce tension, and create a more convivial and amiable atmosphere. With the advent of technology, writing a text message on a mobile phone and showing it to others has become popular as an alternative to whispering!

These days, even some local governments are hosting *goukons* in order to uplift the marriage rate and stop the population decline.

Goukon parties meanwhile are a rapidly growing industry, a hugely proliferating business. You can access all kinds of *goukon* services easily through internet websites.

And for those who are really serious about finding a spouse soon enough, there are also matchmaking services handy. Though marriage seekers in Yahoo! Japan's matchmaking service exceed 1,00,000 entries today, it is just that *goukon* is perhaps more fun.

85

HADAKA NO TSUKIAI

Hadaka no tsukiai in the Japanese lexicon stands for 'naked communion' or 'naked friendship'.

In Japan, it's customary to bathe in shared baths (*sento*/*onsen*), and this is almost always done in your birthday suit. To the Japanese, there is nothing unusual about getting your kit off and jumping in the bath together, although it often makes a lot of tourists blush. Everyone in Japan kind of bathes together – families, friends, even colleagues – and while they bathe, they chat. Conversations range from local gossip to politics, religion to fashion, food to fun. The important thing, however, is that once you are scrubbed clean of the burdens of daily life and soaking in the shared bath, you are naked, and so is your friendship. The common belief is that all barriers are broken down once you are naked, and this is a good opportunity to relax and talk openly with one another.

The Japanese love to take baths. Most Japanese take a bath every day. Not just a shower, but they dip their body into a deep Japanese-style tub filled with hot water.

Most people have their own bath at home, but for the not-so-rich citizens, there are the traditional *sento*, or 'public baths', although their numbers are decreasing rapidly.

The recent fad however is the 'super *sento*', which is increasingly taking the place of the *sento*. 'Super *sento*' is a small complex of baths that consists of various sizes and types, including a jet-bubble jacuzzi and a sauna, combined with a cafeteria, a bar, a hair salon and probably a massage place too.

On top of this, there are countless numbers of *onsen*, or natural hot springs, all over Japan, and visiting these places to take a long soak is one of the most popular and admired Japanese outings since the Edo period.

In hierarchy-conscious Japan, the *hadaka no tsukiai* is a great social leveller. The Japanese people identify themselves very closely with their titles, roles and responsibilities. All the more, taking a bath together, sitting in naked communion gives them the opportunity to lower their defences, forget their social and professional standings and mingle without agenda or ado. They appreciate the opportunity of getting to know each other more openly, and building a 'naked friendship' amongst themselves.

So it is not unusual for work colleagues to choose an *onsen* for their company trip. After a long soak in the hot springs, they gather in a party room where the local delicacies and liquor await them. As they consume the food and the beverages, they are no longer just colleagues but 'naked friends'.

One of the best ways to get to know someone in Japan is to take a bath with them. Stripped of all accoutrements and worldly formalities, the relaxed *onsen* atmosphere gives you the chance to delve deeper. The only other way to cement friendships in Japan is to consume lots of alcohol together. *Hadaka no tsukiai* or *sake*, well the choice is entirely yours.

86

HANABI

The word *hanabi* can be broken into two words; *hana* meaning 'flower' and *bi* meaning 'fire'. *Hanabi* simply means 'fireworks'. *Hanabi* is a Chinese invention. The first appearance of *hanabi* in a Japanese historical document dates back to 1532 AD, when Chinese performers presented a fireworks show before a Japanese aristocrat. According to historical records, those fireworks were not exactly the kind we see today, but something more like a magic show.

The Japanese fireworks of today have their direct origin in the Edo period. Toy fireworks started to appear in the seventeenth century and the first fireworks show for the public took place in 1733 on the bank of Sumida River in Edo (the former name of Tokyo). Barring rare exceptions, these fireworks continue to be held every year, with more and more pomp and show.

Fireworks or *hanabi* in Japan were originally supposed to ward off evil spirits, but over time they became an integral part of

Japanese summers. Today, hundreds of fireworks shows are held every year across the country, mainly during the summer holidays in July and August, attracting hundreds of thousands of spectators. On the other hand, fireworks are not typically used to celebrate New Year, as surprising as it may seem.

The fireworks shells vary in size and intensity, ranging from small inconsequential ones to the world record-holding *Yonshakudama* shells, which are an impressive 1.2 metres in diameter and weigh several hundred kilograms. The most common are star-mines, which are spherical shells that have a variety of burst patterns. The spectacular ones include the famous Niagara sparklers that are usually set under bridges to create the effect of cascading waterfalls. There are also formed shells that burst into familiar shapes such as hearts, smiley faces and cartoon characters.

A secondary attraction of these fireworks is the relaxed festive atmosphere that comes with them. People dress up in *yukata* (the informal cotton *kimono*) and streets are lined with food and game stalls. The firework shows themselves typically start some time after sunset and last for about one to two hours. Many of the longer shows are simply broken up into multiple shorter segments. They often end with a mind-blowing grand finale consisting of hundreds of *hanabi* shells blown up simultaneously. Popular firework shows tend to be very crowded. The competition for good viewing spots can sometimes get obnoxious, and families often show up hours in advance to reserve the best spots for themselves.

Besides the famous public *hanabi*, Japan has also had a culture of toy fireworks. Young parents enjoying toy fireworks with small children in their backyards has become somewhat of a stereotypical summertime scene of a happy Japanese family. But today, birth rates are declining; there are fewer children; children have many other things to do besides playing with toy fireworks; and sadly, young parents can no longer afford a house with a backyard. So, the toy fireworks market is almost dead.

In the last few years, however, there has been a revival of *senkou hanabi,* or 'incense stick fireworks', because of persistent efforts by enthusiasts to recreate and reproduce the delicate sparklers of their childhood.

Hanabi is a visual delight. It is not to be missed if you happen to visit Japan in the summers.

87

HIKIKOMORI

Hikikomori literally means 'pulling inward, being confined'. Manifesting visible symptoms of acute social withdrawal, *hikikomori* are young adults, mostly adolescents, who are reclusive and withdrawn, preferring to be solitary and alone at all times. In fact, their degree of isolation and confinement is extreme. *Hikikomori* refers to both this phenomenon of self-imposed isolation and the recluses themselves. *Hikikomori* are often referred to as loners or 'modern-day hermits'. This neurosis actually accounts for nearly a million Japanese, who seem to be suffering from symptoms of social withdrawal.

Sometimes, for reasons that no one can fully fathom, they just suddenly cut themselves off from the outside world. They lock themselves inside their rooms and refuse to come out to be with friends or family. Their parents then take over their responsibility, feeding them and clothing them, in the hope that, one day, the *hikikomori* sufferer might decide to leave the room!

Most *hikikomori* victims are male, and often tend to be the eldest son. Usually they are schoolchildren who apparently can no longer face the stress of going to school, the pressures to conform and to excel.

Hikikomori is characterized by the individual spending most of their day and nearly every day confined to home; marked and persistent avoidance of social situations, and social withdrawal symptoms causing significant functional impairment. This withdrawal can last beyond six months, and there is, most times, no apparent physical aetiology to account for the social withdrawal symptoms.

No one really knows what triggers *hikikomori*. Some say it is the glorification and nobility of solitude that stretches back to traditional Japanese music, prose and poetry. But this is at best a philosophical view. Some explain its prevalence as originating in the Japanese psychological construct of *amae* (in Freudian terms, 'passive object love', typically of the kind between mother and infant). The Jews, the Italians and the Irish as races are all well-known for having remarkably close mother-son relationships – yet *hikikomori* is without doubt a wholly Japanese phenomenon. The social recluses wish to securely remain in the safety and enduring comfort of the mother's womb.

The dominant nexus of *hikikomori* centres on the period of transformation from youth to the responsibilities and expectations of adult life. In Japan, the transformation of certain susceptible types of youth into mature roles is just not well-handled. Japanese society exerts a great deal of pressure on adolescents to achieve success and to maintain the existing social status quo. As it is social conduct in Japan is extremely demanding, hierarchies are rigid, there is a multitude of expectations; add on to that responsibilities and duties; and the constant pressure to conform. Young adults live in a pressure chamber all the time. And *hikikomori* results.

The phenomenon of *hikikomori* could also be attributed to Japanese parents sending their children to private cram schools, known as *juku*, to 'make up' for lost time. Another source of pressure on Japanese youth is from co-students who may harass and bully (*ijime*) other students for reasons that vary from physical appearance to wealth to academics to athletic performance. Even after graduating from high school or university, many Japanese youth face great difficulties in the job market, ending up with only part-time employment or ending up as freeters (who have foregone the job security of salaried employment) with little income, unable to start a family of their own. All these become contributing factors for *hikikomori*.

Hikikomori is one of Japan's big problems with no real solution in sight.

88

KANJI

❧

A *kanji* in Japan is the quintessential 'party organizer'.
The *kanji* is the one who takes on the responsibility of arranging the *nomikai* (drinking party) at the *izakaya* (restaurant). Most of the time, it is the youngest person of the group (see *senpai kouhai* relationship) who gets to handle the job.

The *kanji*'s tasks are unenviable. He has to decide the invitees (not by himself, but by consensus), fix the date and time, fix the venue, plan the procedure, decide the menu, take care of how the bills are settled, and so on, much like a tour conductor.

Obviously, it is quite different and difficult to be the *kanji* of a big party, like a wedding or a company event, a *bonnenkai*, etc. If the party is very large, professional service providers can be hired and entrusted with the arrangements. If the party is smaller in size, the *kanji* too can relax and partake in the fun with the rest of the group. The most burdensome parties are the ones in between.

Unlike other places, in Japanese parties, one cannot just leave the attendees alone and expect them to have fun. The *kanji* has to plan the procedure and make sure everyone is taken care of, individually and together. The *kanji* puts in great effort to find a good venue, taking into account the preferences of all the participants. He has to think of surprise attractions. He most probably will have to double up as the MC too. It is not an easy job.

But thanks to the internet, the job of the *kanji* has become much less burdensome than in the past. Fixing the date, finding the venue, sending invitations, making reservations, finalizing the menu, all can be done through the computer and the mobile. Making contact and communicating is much easier today than it was in the past.

The task of a *kanji*, with or without the help of technology, is still not smooth. The *kanji* of a *goukon* (matchmaking party), for example, has to put in every effort to decide whom to invite, and then ensure that the invitees do get there, since mingling and meeting is the ultimate purpose of the occasion. So a lot of effort needs to be put into deciding the right list of attendees as those coming to the *goukon* expect to find at least a few, if not all, new faces at the party.

In a *goukon*, the male group invites the female group. It is never the other way around. So the *goukon kanji* has to be a guy with a strong network and outreach, in order to identify and invite a sufficient number of girls to the party. He has to have enough contacts on his radar to choose from. In this case, the *kanji* can thankfully forget senior-junior relationships. The *goukon* group usually consists of people approximately the same age anyway. Merit works. The *kanji* is really there to ensure that there is enough quorum in attendance, everyone is comfortable, the conversations flow. And, of course, there is good food and adequate drink to keep the party in good spirits.

89

KEKKON

Kekkon or 'marriage' is an endangered institution in Japan. The average age of the Japanese males' first marriage is today 30.5, and for females' it is 28.8. This was 25.9 and 23.0 in 1950. The percentage of those unmarried has increased too. It was 8 per cent of the males in the 30–34 age group and 5.7 per cent of females of the same age group in 1950. As of 2010, this had increased to a surprising 47.3 per cent and 37.5 per cent respectively.

Traditionally, marriages were categorized into two types according to the method of finding a partner – *omiai*, meaning arranged or resulting from an arranged introduction, and *ren'ai*, in which the prospective husband and wife met and decided to marry on their own – although the distinction has grown less meaningful over the post-war decades as Western ideas of love altered the Japanese perception of marriage.

Reasons for the institution waning in Japan may vary. But it is the ever-changing social structure that is at the core of this phenomenon.

Reason No. 1: Today, more females are involved in serious career development. Meanwhile, there isn't enough social infrastructure to support the domestic chores of married career women. So, women postpone marriage for as long as is possible.

Reason No. 2: Since lifetime employment and the seniority system have become almost obsolete, young males' futures are hard to predict. Probably women today decide to wait just a little longer to see how the careers of their potential partners are shaping up, before agreeing to tie the knot.

Reason No. 3: Young males (and females) do not find any tangible benefit from marriage any longer. In the cities, there are all kinds of convenient services to support a very comfortable single lifestyle. So, why bother?

Reason No. 4: There is an increasing population of low-wage workers and jobless youngsters. The troubled economic situation is making marriage impossible for people at the bottom of the pyramid. The increasing numbers of freelancers and temporary workers have no security for their future. Obviously, they make bad potential grooms.

Reason No. 5: Matchmaking opportunities for arranged marriages are almost absent today. Although the opportunities for young people to meet persons of the opposite sex look aplenty on the surface, the fact is, receding ties with families, relatives and local communities are eliminating any chances of matchmaking which effectively worked in the past.

Reason No. 6: Lessening pressure. In the old days, parents, relatives, neighbours, co-workers, practically everybody around you would put pressure to get married if you started to approach the age of thirty. Now, one doesn't hear anything of the sort.

Reason No. 7: Too much noise in the media, on the internet, as well as in daily conversations of unhappy marriages, growing divorce rates and singles staying single.

Some of the above reasons may be common with other countries around the world, but are a little more acutely felt in Japan. Almost 90 per cent of unmarried Japanese intend to marry, and yet the percentage of people who don't continues to grow. Surveys also show a declining interest in dating and sexual relationships among young people, especially men. As per a study put out by the government recently, women in their early twenties had a one in four chance of never marrying, and a two in five chance of remaining childless. Marriage is surely in trouble in Japan.

90

KIKUBARI

*K*ikubari is a combination of two words. *Kubaru*, meaning to 'spread around' and *ki*, meaning 'life force or attention'.

There is no exact equivalent of *kikubari* in English. Perhaps the closest is 'pay attention to other people', but somehow this does not capture its nuance. The one basic assumption behind *kikubari* is that everyone is part of a community. This community may be your co-workers, your subordinates, your customers, or any other stakeholders whose needs you should be attuned to. By doing *kikubari*, you try to understand the needs and desires of these people by paying careful attention, and by anticipation, so you can pre-empt whatever they may want. Acting on that knowledge, you are able to comport yourself in such a way that not only avoids irritating them, but actively delights them.

Because the Japanese are so habituated to operating in groups, *kikubari* is nearly an unconscious activity for them. A Japanese person who does not do *kikubari* would be considered a poor group member, lacking in an essential soft skill for getting along with others. A vendor who cannot do *kikubari* would surely have unhappy customers, and a superior in a team who cannot do *kikubari* would have subordinates with low motivation.

Kikubari has also sometimes been defined in Japan as 'the art of anticipation'. It can be recognized as the Japanese style of silent, pre-emptive and unprompted customer service that anticipates needs as a base level of service. Let us suppose you are in the Ginza business district of Tokyo. And let us presume you have time on your hands. You walk for about twenty to twenty-five minutes in the sticky heat of Japan's late-July summer to meet someone at the Imperial hotel. Your business associate has not yet arrived. Meanwhile, an alert and observant clerk on duty at the check-in counter notices the sweat on your brow, and takes it upon themselves to serve you a glass of iced barley tea and to bring you a chilled *oshibori* towel. They anticipate your needs and fulfill them proactively, the ultimate in Japanese-style customer service.

Kikubari is also at the heart of Japanese design. Actually, true customer-centric design which prioritises all decision-making on customer needs. The Japanese observe and truly understand how people use products and services, and spare no effort to accommodate their expectations in pursuing the design effort. Simple and useful examples can be identified from day-to-day life. Squeezable ketchup bottles came from such observations and replaced the cumbersome glass bottles. So also the concept of perforated butter! Yes, pre-cut butter so you can have the perfect portion of butter every single time.

It is said that Konosuke Matsushita of Panasonic was a great believer in the virtue and value of *kikubari*. He observed the cardinal rule that any customer who was dissatisfied with a product needed to be shown even more consideration and politeness than what he received at the time of initial purchase, taking after-sales service at his company to unparalleled levels of customer satisfaction, even joy. Making customers die-hard fans of the brand, and even converting those who had a problem with a Panasonic product into lifetime loyalists.

91

OGORI/WARIKAN

Ogori and *warikan* are two separate words. *Ogori* means 'treat'. *Warikan* means 'even split'.

When the Japanese go out for dinner in a group, the bill will at most times be split evenly among the members of the group. This is called *warikan*. It's a typical case of the burden-sharing spirit of the Japanese.

On the face of it, it looks like a fair enough deal, but is not necessarily so. First of all, the financial status of each member of the group may vary. The burden is heavier on the less affluent. And the amount of food and beverage one consumes can vary from person to person. So what if one guy in the group is rich, and eats and drinks a lot? Well, then an evenly split *warikan* doesn't sound fair then, does it?

But not to worry. The Japanese have worked out all the possible tactical adjustments to resolve such issues in *warikan*.

1. Seniority Ladder Split: In this case, the older one pays more. This method is based on the assumption that the older member earns more, which may not always be true but is generally an acceptable assumption at most times. This is a popular method of settling the bill as it keeps the *senpai kouhai*, or 'senior-junior', culture intact. Calculating and deciding the amount each person pays is the job of the *kanji* or the party organizer.

2. Basic Package Split: This is self-explanatory. The first round of food and beverage, pre-ordered by the *kanji*, will be evenly split while the additional orders will be on each person individually. One could improvise on this one. The food bill could be evenly split, while drinks can be on each member individually. An evenly split basic charge could be collected in advance. Fixed price buffet could be arranged until a certain hour. This often works.

3. The All-You-Can-Drink Package: A few restaurants offer such fixed-price packages which allow you to choose from a surprisingly wide range of beverages on the menu. One can drink as much as one likes within a set hour: probably two to three hours. This is a much-preferred choice.

But no matter what, there is always the hint of unfairness in the division of the bill. But that really is notional. The Japanese just will always 'go Dutch', a few Yen more or a few Yen less. What is interesting, however, is that while this *warikan* practice is near universal at dinner, at lunch everyone surprisingly pays their own bill. Peculiar, but true.

Different rules apply if it's a treat, or *ogori*. If the dinner has some kind of special significance attached to it, such as a celebration of a pitch well done or the welcoming of someone from afar, it becomes a 'treat' by the host of the occasion. If one person is senior to the rest of the group, he would normally take care of the bill. This is called *ogori*. And most of the time, such a treat would get billed to the company of the host, much like the entertainment expense of a head honcho elsewhere.

92

SHINSOTSU MUSHOKU

Shinsotsu mushoku in English translates to a 'recent graduate with no job'.

This corresponds to a Japanese colloquialism 'freeter'. Freeter, a composite of English and German, is actually an abbreviation for 'free arbeiter', which refers to a person who takes up casual work in a carefree manner. As the term implies, 'freeter' refers to those who do not actively seek employment and enter society without taking up a fixed source of income. Despite having graduated from high school or university, 'freeters' opt for a free-and-easy lifestyle, supported by casual work with no more than 800-1000 Yen in income per hour.

These young people who do not have any inclination to find a steady job are frequently found in large cities. This observation is supported by the results of a survey of graduates from Tokyo metropolitan high schools, which showed that 20 per cent graduates aspire to become a 'freeter'. The number of university graduates who aspire to become 'freeters' also shows an upward trend and one that is expected to continue in the future. It has been reported that as many as 2.5 million youth currently fall into this category. The social background behind the increase of 'freeters' is the decrease in the number of new job openings due to the prolonged economic slump. However, the prominence of recent beliefs (for example, 'I do not want to do a job that I don't like', 'I can live without having a steady job these days', or 'I want to give priority to what I want to do rather than work when I am young') is also an important factor in the upsurge of 'freeters'.

'Freeters' as a category have close parallels with what are described as NEETs (Not in Education, Employment or Training) in the UK. NEETs, much like 'freeters', are young people with low educational qualifications, with no ready intention to pick a job and with little or no vocational training that could become a job enabler.

Back in Japan, there is a related term, 'parasite single', created by the sociologist Yamada Masahiro, which has become widely used in reference to those members of the young generation who enjoy their single-hood, while continuing to live with their parents and receive partial financial support from them. Typically, these individuals fail to become independent and do not marry, even after the age of thirty. According to Yamada's estimate, the number of 'parasite singles' in Japan is more than 10 million. The social background behind the increase of 'parasite singles' is a widespread desire amongst the young Japanese to avoid the hardships associated with moving out of the family home and becoming independent. The rise in 'parasite singles' has also been suggested as one of the main reasons for the continuing fall in the birth rate.

You don't have to look far in Japan for inspiration to become a 'freeter'. Japanese culture traditionally praises people who live to work (rather than the other way around), yet the country's bookshelves are filling up with books with titles which loosely translate into *Why Do We Work? Job-Switching King, Manual for a Happy Jobless Life,* and *Timetable for Quitting a Company* (illustrative names). The times, they are a changing …

93

SUKOSHI DEKIMASU

Sukoshi dekimasu actually means 'I can do a little'. So, when you want to say, 'I can speak a little Japanese' you say, '*nihongo ga sukoshi dake dekimasu,*' where *dekimasu* means 'to be able to'.

Japan is particularly inert when it comes to speaking or understanding the English language. Actually, this is an unfair statement to make. Most kids in Japan are taught the English language from junior school. But since everyone converses and communicates in Japanese only, the English language is rarely used. And this non-use of the language tends to make their English rusty and patchy.

As a foreigner in Japan, this can be extremely frustrating. To naturally presume that English is the universal *lingua franca* is an assumption best, and quickly, dispensed with. You cannot, most times, ask even basic questions to a bystander or to the girl at the counter. Your questions are more often than not met with a blank stare or a half smile, followed by an apology, 'Me no speak English'. It is not that the Japanese *cannot* speak English. It is simply that they *will not* speak English. Given time, the average Japanese, especially in the more cosmopolitan Tokyo, can manage a somewhat awkward conversation. It is just that it takes more time for them to choose the words in their mind, string them together, phrase a sentence, and then express themselves cogently and coherently. In the process, many of the Japanese tend to become self-conscious and abandon the effort to avoid the embarrassment of making a mistake, or more importantly, a fool of themselves.

All of this becomes even more befuddling when you do business in, and with, Japan. Well-drafted mails or letters in English can sometimes receive no answers, or you receive an unintelligible response in Japanese that cannot be fathomed or deciphered.

Rather than get frustrated or dismayed, it is easy to operate in Japan with a simple set of rules. When using public transport or a cab, get the hotel concierge to write your destination in Japanese on a piece of paper. This would make communication simple and uncomplicated. If going out shopping, it is best to use the calculator to check the price. No ambiguity then. For food, just memorize key words, such as *mizu*, the Japanese for 'water'. So a request for 'cold water' would be '*Tsumetai mizu*'. *Yakitori* for 'chicken'. *Gohan* for 'rice', actually 'cooked rice'. And, of course, the basic courtesies: *kon'nichiwa* for 'hello', *ohay gozaimasu* for 'good morning', *oyasumi nasai* for 'good night', *sumimasen!* for 'I'm sorry!' (most frequently used in Japan, also interchangeable with 'excuse me'), *sayonara* for 'good-bye', and the finer (actually the more practical) nuances like *moshi moshi* which is the 'telephone hello' and not *kon'nichiwa*.

Always get important letters and presentations translated into Japanese and send them ahead of the meeting. Use your English deck while having the Japanese one on the other side. And, of course, all formal meetings warrant an interpreter, especially one who would not merely translate words, but communicate thinking. Such detailing invariably yields positive results.

Sukoshi dekimasu is actually a mindset. A very deep-rooted Japanese mindset. To survive and thrive in Japan, you have to learn to circumvent it, not get scared by it!

VII

SPIRITUAL

94

EMA

❧

*E**ma* (picture horse) are small specially made wooden plaques on which worshippers of the Shinto faith write their prayers and wishes to god. The *ema* are then left hanging up at the shrine, where the *kami* (spirits or gods) are believed to receive them.

Ema is made up of two *kanjis*: one for the picture, and the other for the horse. Horses were revered as the vehicles of gods in early Japan. It was customary for worshippers to donate horses to shrines in the belief that the deities would be more inclined to listen to their wishes then. But horses were expensive. So visitors instead started to donate horses made of clay, wood, and paper. From this the wooden plaque with the image of a horse upon them was born.

Everyone is free to purchase an *ema* board outside a shrine and make a wish. The boards usually cost as little as 500 to 1000 Yen, and can be bought at the little divinity shops that also sell *omamori* (lucky charms). Usually, there is an attendant at the shop to serve and collect money. But smaller shrines invariably leave the items out on display, and there is a self-serve box to place the money in. Everything is clearly priced, and all donations go towards the upkeep of the shrine. As for making the actual wish, there are no specific rules. You just need to pick up a pen and write on the blank side of the *ema*. This ensures that you do not spoil the pretty art on the front. However, some people prefer to write the wish over the picture, and put their name and address on the blank side. Personal details are not mandatory and just a nickname with a mention of your town or city is enough. You also don't need to know Japanese; you can write your wish in your native language. Big, popular shrines (such as *Meiji* in Tokyo or *Fushimi Inari* in Kyoto) have ema written in many different languages by visitors.

Ema prayers are most commonly for health, love, safe childbirth, and career success. Around exam time, many students and parents wish and pray for luck and good results. Being common, they are referred to as *goukaku*, and fill the *ema* displays. Lots of students also include cute artwork along with their wishes, so they are worth a look at, from a touristy perspective!

After you've purchased your *ema* board, written your wish, what do you do with it? Well, hang it up! All shrines have specific areas demarcated for the display of *ema*. This could either be a board with hooks to hang the *ema*, or even an entire wall, depending on the size of the shrine.

So what happens to your *ema* left hanging outside the shrine? The *ema* continue to be displayed on the board until *Hatsumode* (usually the first shrine visit following the New Year, normally between 1 and 3 January), after which they are ceremonially burned, along with the *omamori* from the year gone by (*omamori* have a validity of just one year, post which they need to be replaced. Old *omamori* are discarded at the shrines when new *omamori* are purchased). This usually happens around 15 January. This ceremony is known as *Otakiage*. When the *ema* and *omamori* are burned in the sacred fire, prayers are supposed to help the wishes come true.

95

ENGIDEMONAI

Engidemonai is actually a phrase, not one word, and can be broken down into *engi* and *demonai*. *Engi* is a noun that comes from the Buddhist concept of 'consequence'. *Demonai,* on the other hand, is a verb form of negation. So literally, *engidemonai* means something like, 'I denounce your mentioning the words of bad consequence'. Or, simply put, the very mention of bad luck brings bad luck.

The Japanese are a superstitious race. There is an actual belief, widely prevalent, that if you even refer to possible bad luck, it could actually bring you real bad luck as a consequence! If you were at an airport sending off your Japanese friend and said something like, 'Don't worry. The chances of an air crash in modern times are just 0.0001 per cent!' Although it is meant to be a little joke, just to make light-hearted conversation, he would surely not like it. His startled response would most likely be, *'Engidemonai!* The mention of bad luck brings bad luck!'

It is because of this superstition that the Japanese hesitate to discuss the worst-case scenario of projects, which some say makes them vulnerable to surprise attacks and disasters. The Japanese show remarkable patience and resilience once the mishaps occur, but may not be so good at preparing for them in advance. *Souteigai*, or 'beyond expectation', was the buzzword in the Japanese media after the Fukushima nuclear power plant was hit by the tsunami of 11 March 2011. The common verdict in the media was that Fukushima was very poorly prepared for the catastrophe because no one had really talked about it or even discussed it, believing it to be a bad omen to have such conversations before the disaster actually happened.

This tendency not to face the worst possibilities as likely eventualities, and clinging on to wishful thinking, makes the Japanese energetic explorers in the good times. But explorers who are not well prepared for the worst-case scenarios are reckless by definition, aren't they? It may therefore be surprising to note that the normally risk-averse Japanese, who get into detailed preparation for everything, somehow fall into a black hole when it comes to actual risk planning. It is here that the superstition of *engidemonai* manifests itself. It is almost as if just thinking of negative outcomes will actually trigger them into happening, and hence it is better not to even think of them, let alone prepare for them.

Like every country, Japan has its quota of unique and sometimes weird superstitions, from unlucky sleeping positions to elaborate rituals which curse the people you dislike and help you settle scores. For example, there is a practice in Japan called *ushi no koku mairi* where people visit a shrine during the 'hour of the ox' (1–3 am). They bring with them a straw doll known as a *waranigyou* that represents the person who will suffer the curse and use a long nail called a *gosunkugi* to nail the doll to the shrine's holy tree. Wherever the nail strikes the doll, it is supposed to bring pain to those parts of the cursed person's body!

96

HAKA JIMAI

Haka jimai stands for 'grave closing'.

Most Japanese families used to have their private family graves. Well, they still do, but times are changing. Most families are considering *haka jimai*, or 'grave closing', due to a variety of reasons.

The foremost reason, of course, is the fragmentation of families. Young nuclear families are not as close to their parents as the older generations were. Ageing fathers are finding it difficult to persuade their sons to take care of the family graves. The ever-declining birthrate is making things even worse. The maintenance costs of the graves can be prohibitive depending on their location. And this scares the children away.

Earlier, the graveyards were owned by Buddhist temples, which were supported by donations from the grave-owner families. Old family relationships with the temples continue, but not all members of the family today are inclined to pay for and support these old graves, since they have other priorities to take care of in life. Dwindling support from patron families is making the upkeep of these graves a problem for Buddhist temples.

Another reason is the diversification in funeral-styles. Japanese funerals used to be mostly Buddhist, but now, many choose to do it their own way. Some keep the cremated remnants of the dead at home, others scatter them in forests or the sea. In fact, today there are many modern, computer-controlled, religion-free cinerarium buildings around the country storing thousands of cremated ashes in pots.

The high prices of funeral plots, costing on an average 2 million Yen, have led to a new service of Grave Apartments (*ohaka no manshon*), where a locker-sized grave can be purchased for about 400,000 Yen. Some of these may even include new-fangled features like a touchscreen displaying a picture of the deceased, messages from the family and friends, a family tree, and other such information. Due to the cost of land, a graveyard in Tokyo has recently been opened by a temple in floors three to eight of a nine-storeyed building, where the lower floors are for funeral ceremonies.

But *haka jimai* itself is not that easy.

If a Japanese person has a long-standing relationship with the temple where he has his family grave, closing it will surely not make the temple happy. In most cases, they ask for unbelievably high closing fees. There is a ritual ceremony to ease the spirits of the dead. And demolition costs have to be paid too.

The practice of *haka jimai* could well signify that the Japanese are becoming less religious and more economy-conscious. But if economy were the only concern, they could just stop visiting the grave and refuse to pay the maintenance fee. Cemeteries can't come and arrest them! After a death, cemeteries may try to identify who has inherited the grave, but once they decide that the grave is completely abandoned, it will be demolished by the cemetery after some time and the space will be sold to someone else. So it's not like the grave owners are not closing the graves because they are no longer religious. On the contrary, they are still religious deep-down and afraid of possible ominous consequences of abandoning them without proper rituals. Hence, *haka jimai*.

97

ONI WA SOTO!

Oni wa soto translates into 'Devil, go out!'

But to understand the expression, its context, and significance, one has to delve deeper to appreciate its true import.

The third day of February is called *Setsubun* in Japan. Although it is not a national holiday, the day has a lot of traditional value placed on it. *Setsubun* in Japan is the 'bean-throwing festival' or 'bean-throwing ceremony', and is usually the day before the commencement of spring. The following day, 4 February, is called *Rissyun*, which literally means the beginning of spring.

On *Setsubun,* people take part in a traditional *mame-maki* ceremony. They throw roasted soybeans (*mame*) and shout '*Oni wa soto! Fuku wa uti* (Get out, devil! Come in, happiness)!'. Or shout '*Oni wa soto! Fuku wa uchi!*' meaning 'Devil, go out! Fortune, come in!' After the ceremony, in order to get happiness in the coming year, each person is obliged to eat the number of beans equal to their age. Another traditional custom is putting a head of a sardine and *hiiragi* on the door to get rid of *oni* (ogre/devil). In the olden days, someone in the household wore a mask and played the part of *oni*. Other members chased him around the house, throwing soy beans at him.

As part of the ceremony, the Japanese also usually eat an *Ehomaki*, which is a kind of *makizushi*, on *Setsubun*. *Makizushi* means 'call over happiness'. It is usually eaten without cutting because if it is cut, it implies a 'break-up'. The Japanese usually put seven kinds of ingredients in the *Ehomaki* after the seven gods of fortune. They then eat it without saying a word. Generally, it's because it would be rude to the gods if someone were talking while eating. In a slight variation to this ceremony, people living in the Kansai area eat *Nori Maki* (a special sushi roll) while facing the 'lucky direction' and not saying a word. Same ceremonies, minor localization.

If you look closely, there is something odd, or at least very unusual, about this ritual phrase, '*Oni wa soto! Fuku wa uchi!*' It doesn't imply any wish to eliminate the devil, but just hopes the devil will go out of the house. Such dichotomy of out-ness versus in-ness is a key to deciphering the enigma of Japanese culture. In a different part of this book, there is reference to the phase '*uchinokaisha*' or 'our company'. This '*uchi*' is the same '*uchi*' in the phrase, '*Fuku wa uchi!*' The literal translation of this particular word *uchi* is 'inside'. The Japanese people may be polite and hospitable to foreigners, but never show their true feelings until the foreigner penetrates the barrier and becomes an insider. Very, very few do.

As a visitor to Japan, you have little choice but to remain an outsider. They will call you *gaijin* or 'outside-men', and treat you like a wonderful guest from outer space. The '*gai*' in *gaijin* is an alternative way to read the same Chinese character as the *soto* in '*Oni wa soto!*' So much for sympathy for the devil!

VIII

SPORTS AND RECREATION

98

ISSYOKENMEI

Issyokenmei ganbarimasu is 'to devote one's life to just one thing'. You will often hear this phrase coming from a young Japanese declaring his eagerness at the start of a new job. Literally, *issyo* means one place. *Kenmei* means to stake one's life. *Ganbarimasu* means 'I will do my best'. Put together, it means, 'I will stake my life for the job'.

The Japanese put high value on one's devotion to one thing. The ones who show their talent in various fields at once are often perceived as untrustworthy. In America, for example, there are some baseball players who play football in the off-season. In Japan, this is unthinkable. While American pragmatism allows people to do whatever they want as long as the efforts bring certain results, in Japan, the attitude of devotion is equally, or sometimes more, important than the result.

This spiritual tendency of a lifetime devotion in many ways is perhaps the hidden reason that prevents Japanese working men from job-hopping. It is true that the vestiges of a lifetime employment system are still around, but that doesn't explain why freelancers, whether a cook, a mechanic or an artist, who devote themselves to just one vocation for their lifetime, are so admired.

A man devoting his life to his vocation is one of the typical stereotypes favoured in the country. From documentaries to dramas to cartoons, you will find the same type of endeavouring heroes on screen. Did you, for example, know that the *Suraj: The Rising Star*, the cartoon TV drama of an Indian boy who devotes himself to becoming a pro-cricket player some day, was the adaptation of a Japanese cartoon about baseball?

Ichiro, a Japanese right fielder playing in American Major League Baseball since 2001, is the hero of all heroes in Japan. Besides the fact that he is the first, and so far only, Japanese player who has accomplished so much as to be assured a place in the American Baseball Hall of Fame, his legendary devotion to his job is much admired in Japan. His training is said to be perfectly planned out, and according to his own testimony, he goes through the same menu day after day, month after month, year after year. He says, 'Unless you stay doing the same thing over and over again, you cannot tell the repercussion of small changes from time to time.' He adds, 'You can reach a far distance only by accumulating small steps of everyday life.' He is the embodiment of the ideal Japanese working ethic.

Issyokenmei can also be translated as 'to work very hard at something'. The roots of this phrase come from a Samurai's way of life, literally translated as guarding one's land at all costs. Today, many martial arts organizations use this term as a way of saying students should completely devote themselves to every action they take. Focus and devotion are therefore the mantras to success both in the short run, as well as for the long term.

99

KANKOU

*K*ankou means 'tourism'. And travel is in the life blood of the Japanese. They just love to wander the world.

Tosa Nikki was the first Japanese diary-style travelogue, which was written in the tenth century, a journal of the nobleman Ki No Tsurayuki on his travels from Tosa (current Kochi Prefecture) to Kyoto. Prominent poets like Saigyo and Basho also wrote about their travels, stringing the narrations into verse. In the late Edo period (early nineteenth century), Juppensha Ikku wrote a comic novel depicting the episodes of an odd couple travelling along the Tokaido highway. This novel became one of the biggest bestsellers of its time. Tourism was a big distraction among the Japanese populace by then. Pilgrimage to the Ise Shrine was said to be a thing one ought to do at least once in a lifetime. Today's favourite tourist spots like Kamakura and Enoshima were already favourites even a couple of centuries ago. There were travel agencies too that could arrange travel for tourists. Guidebooks were available. So, *kankou* is not new to Japan.

Travel both within Japan and outside the country is equally popular. The domestic trips of the Japanese (overnight trip or longer) add up to more than 300 million every year. About 1.5 million Japanese travel outside of the country every month, totalling about 18 million a year. Japanese television is full of travel programmes covering both domestic and international destinations. Because the Japanese are so much 'on-the-go', bullet trains, planes and highways are always crowded. However, since 2000, growth rates in the travel industry have somehow plateaued. The year-on-year growth that tourism was witnessing post the Second World War and during the boom, now seems a thing of the past. Which is not to say that the Japanese have started to travel less. It is just that the population is growing older.

The oldest historical monument, the newest art gallery, the tallest mountain, the most-fashionable afternoon tea, the longest-running musical – Japanese tourists are big fans of ticking off the most famous sites in whichever destination they find themselves, often researching meticulously in advance. Shopping is another highlight – not only for big name designer clothing, but also for kilos of *omiyage* souvenirs, which they will selflessly lug home for colleagues, neighbours, family and friends.

The international travelling ambitions of the Japanese tourist often err on the romantic side – Liverpool for The Beatles-lovers, the Lake District for Beatrix Potter readers, Hawaii for a taste of old-school island paradise, Barcelona for its architecture and creativity, Paris for its poetry, fashion and cuisine. It is interesting to note that the so-called Paris Syndrome – that surreally perplexing psychological condition which hits visitors when they find that real-life Paris is not the stuff of their dreams – afflicts mainly Japanese travellers.

In 2013, Mt Fuji was declared a World Heritage site, and Tokyo is set to host the 2020 Olympics. Japan is now looking forward to more and more visitors coming in from overseas, rather than just the Japanese travelling to foreign shores.

100

MAN-IN-ON-REI

Man-In-On-Rei is 'Thank you, the house is full' in Japanese. Were you to go to a Sumo wrestling tournament, in the festive and festooned atmosphere, you may see four banners hanging from the ceiling facing different directions. On the banners, four Chinese characters would be written: *Man-In-On-Rei*. These are celebratory banners proclaiming, 'Thank you, the house is full'.

Man-In-On-Rei is not a phrase exclusively used at Sumo tournaments alone. In the Edo period, when theatrical culture for common people blossomed, they hung *Man-In-On-Rei* banners whenever the theatres were full. On such occasions, theatre owners handed small amounts of cash to staff members to show them their gratitude. The money was in a small envelope called *Ooiri Bukuroor,* or 'Big Crowd Envelope.'

You can still witness the practice in *Kabuki* and *Yose* theatres today. A full house deserves some self-congratulatory chest thumping, doesn't it?

For the first time in twenty-one years, *Man-In-On-Rei* banners were hung at Sumo tournaments throughout the year 2017. One tournament lasts for fifteen days and there are six tournaments in a year. That counts to ninety days in a row. Ninety days therefore of sold-out tickets and full houses. The display of *Man-In-On-Rei* banners indicates that the sport and its fans are in good fiddle.

The banner over the suspended roof reading *Man-In-On-Rei* is a good omen and means a full house is in attendance during the *honbasho* (tournament). This banner is lowered after the *Juryo* (second-highest division) bouts are finished, the moment the *ki* (wooden clappers) signal the beginning of the Makuuchi (highest division) bouts. It is said that the banner is only shown if at least 80 per cent of the admission tickets for that day are sold by 3 pm.

Sumo has gone through tough years in the past twenty-odd years. It was almost considered an obsolete sport, anachronistic in context and no longer relevant to modern times. It had become difficult to attract younger audiences. A gamble scandal in 2010 also didn't help matters.

But in the past few years, female audiences kept growing due to the debut of young and attractive Sumo wrestlers one after another, giving a fillip and a new hope to the sport.

Another big attraction has been the arrival of a Japanese *yokozuna,* or champion, for the first time in nearly twenty years. *Yokozuna* Kisenosato won fourteen out of fifteen matches in the first tournament of the year 2017. Until then, all the champions for years had been Mongolians. The return of the Japanese as champions to the *honbasho* (official professional Sumo tournament) has ignited renewed interest in Sumo wrestling.

But diversions and mishaps continue to plague the sport. While it looked that all was finally well with Sumo as a sport, another scandal occurred a couple of years ago, clouding all the good news that had been coming in. One Mongolian champion allegedly attacked another Mongolian wrestler in a closed-door party one night during an exhibition match tour. This happened just at the beginning of the November tournament, but thankfully did not affect the audience attendance. It was *Man-In-On-Rei* until the end!

Similarly, *Man-In-On-Rei* is happening with the *Kabuki* theatre too. Once seen almost as obsolete, the performances are now attracting younger crowds. Happy days are here again!

101

SHOUGI

Shougi is a traditional Japanese game which resembles chess. It is played between two players. At the start of the game, each player has twenty wedge-shaped *Shougi* pieces displayed on each side of the wooden board of nine-by-nine squares. And the goal is to move the pieces alternately and checkmate the opponent's king.

Shougi has a long history of more than a thousand years. But it gained national recognition and prominence when newspapers started to cover the matches of high-ranking players in the beginning of the twentieth century.

Shougi has had its ups and downs in terms of popularity. But all of a sudden, *Shougi* became the centre of attention in Japan in 2017 when a fourteen-year-old prodigy, Sota Fujii, won a record twenty-nine straight matches starting from his debut as a professional. His debut match was in December 2016, when he defeated the oldest top-ranked player, Hifumi Kato, aged seventy-seven, who was himself a child prodigy at the time of his debut.

Sota Fujii has become a national hero of sorts, and consequently his fame and fandom has gone beyond *Shougi* enthusiasts. *Shougi* kit sales have skyrocketed; digital versions of *Shougi* too are selling like hot cakes on the net. Children's *Shougi* classes are receiving more applications than they can accept. Meanwhile, Sota Fujii has become a national obsession. His eating habits and his every meal are recorded faithfully by the media; his favourite toy as an infant is a hit product nationally; his clothes, his bags, his everything is being copied and sold to a Japanese public high on this *Shougi* sensation. This has also given fillip to official goods, stationary, T-shirts and more being marketed by the Japan *Shougi* Association, so phenomenal is the *Shougi* fever in Japan.

It was not only Sota Fujii's record that marked 2017 as a special year in *Shougi* history. There were two other surprising pieces of news.

One was that a *Shougi Meijin* title holder was defeated by AI (Artificial Intelligence) for the first time. The *Shougi* champion, Amahiko Sato, was challenged to a match against a computer in May 2017, and he lost.

In December 2017, in what was probably the biggest news in the world of *Shougi*, even dwarfing the exploits of Sota Fujii, came the news that Yoshiharu Habu had become the first person in *Shougi* history to qualify as a lifetime holder of all seven of Japan's major *Shougi* titles by earning a Lifetime *Ryuo* qualification with his seventh *Ryuo* tournament victory that December. There was jubilation in the world of *Shougi,* with extensive coverage on television and with *Shougi* dominating news headlines for days.

Presently, *Shougi* is at the height of its popularity in Japan. Many who didn't even think of *Shougi* until now are starting to play it.

Those who have no plan to play still keep their eyes on *Shougi* news so as not to be left out of the conversation.

Hifumi Kato, whom Sota Fujii defeated at his debut match, meanwhile retired in June 2017. Despite his defeat, he has become a TV star because of his charming character and the enduring Japanese appetite for *Shougi*.

102

SUMO

❧

The characters of *Sumo* or *Sumou* literally mean 'striking one another'.

It is a world-renowned, competitive full-contact Japanese wrestling sport where a *rikishi* (wrestler) attempts to force another wrestler out of a circular ring (*dohyō*), or forces him into touching the ground with anything except the soles of his feet.

Sumo wrestling continues to be one of the most popular professional sports in Japan. The rules are quite simple. Two wrestlers grapple with each other in the ring made out of clay to either throw the opponent to the ground or to push him out of the ring. The huge wrestlers wear nothing but a traditional top knot on their head and a piece of loincloth. The fifteen-day long tournament is held every other month, starting January. That means there are six tournaments a year: three in Tokyo and the rest in three other big cities. More than thirty matches held each day and broadcast live on TV throughout the country.

Despite its simple appearance, Sumo wrestling is quite deep in terms of technique and tactics, which have been nurtured through its long history of approximately 1500 years. Sumo wrestling actually started in ancient times as a ritual. The symbolic salt of purification thrown by the wrestlers before each match is probably one ritual remnant of it. Professional Sumo wrestling itself appeared in the Edo period (1603–1868 AD). It gained national popularity after a TV station started to air the matches in the 1950s.

There was a time when most Japanese youngsters aspired to join Sumo wrestling. But today, despite its popularity and the big money involved, it is getting somewhat difficult to recruit young wrestlers to the sport. As a consequence, many of the star players in the Sumo league are now foreigners. The two grand champions are Mongolians. Besides those two, twelve Mongolians are in the top two *Makuuchi* and *Juryou* ranks. There are also two Bulgarians, two Georgians, one Russian, one Chinese, one Czech, one Brazilian, and one Egyptian in the rankings.

The Egyptian wrestler, Oosunaarashi or 'Great Sandstorm', who retired in March 2018 (after being involved in a traffic accident when he was driving without a valid licence), for example, became the hot stock of the Sumo world a few years back. He was the first Muslim Sumo wrestler in its entire history. He was an amateur Sumo champion in Egypt, a student majoring in accounting, but he left Egypt in the summer of 2011 after the revolution took place. His professional Sumo wrestling debut in Japan was in 2012. His first tournament after he was speed promoted to the *Juryou* rank took place in July 2013, coinciding with the holy month of Ramadan. He fought fifteen matches without eating all day (the Sumo tournament is held in the afternoon and ends at around

6 pm). Despite such adverse conditions, he won ten matches out of fifteen, which is surely an achievement for such a new wrestler.

Sumo is still moored in its religious origins. Shinto principles rule the everyday lives of the Sumo wrestlers. Each of the ring-entering ceremonies, for example, is a Shinto purification ritual; and every newly promoted *yokozuna* (the highest rank in Sumo) is obligated to perform his first ring-entering ceremony at the Meiji Shrine in Tokyo.

ACKNOWLEDGEMENTS

Japan Made Easy took me eight years to finish. I started to write the book in 2011. At first, it seemed like a breeze. I thought I had it all in my head. But once I got into actually researching every Japanese word and phrase I wanted to include in the book, it became tougher and tougher to manage the language, the interpretations, the nuances and the very many shades that each word or phrase could mean in Japan. I trailed off after the first few weeks. Resumed writing maybe a year later. Meandered off again. Almost exited. Then started again. Then again. And again.

I reached out to Jun Nakano, my old friend and colleague from Dentsu. Nakano san was not just supportive and helpful, but actually became the anchor for all my writings. In the process I also discovered a hidden talent of his which I was completely unaware of despite knowing him for years. It turned out that Nakano san is a fabulous illustrator ... and all the 101 illustrations in this book are entirely his contribution. Nakano san has been the guiding spirit, the man who lighted up the path as I trudged along writing and re-writing almost every piece, conveying his grudging approval to some of my writings, disagreeing with many, and junking quite a few. A big thank you to him for his time, his wisdom and his honest feedback, always.

My childhood friend, Prof. Avanindra (Abu) Chopra read every word of my initial manuscript. He changed, chopped, edited, added, deleted and replaced more words than I had actually perhaps written! Abu is the world's most meticulous teacher of the English language and any departures from *Wren & Martin* offend and agitate him. He brought discipline and rigour to my writings. Abu, you are a wonder, buddy!

My sister, Dr Anurag Yadav, the one who has inherited the genius gene in the family, read through every word of my manuscript and pointed out errors and inconsistencies I had completely missed or overlooked. Balloo: you are the best.

While they may have had nothing to directly do with the writing of this book, all my various friends and seniors from Dentsu actually taught me most of what I have written in *Japan Made Easy* during interactions at work, but mostly after-hours. Narita san, Mataki san, Takashima san, Ishii san, Kato san, Niimura san, Kobuse san, Ueno san, Yoshitome san, Takahashi san, Yamamura san, Matsushima san, Harada san, Ishibashi san, Tsuruda san, Terasawa san, Baba san ... they hosted me multiple times in Tokyo, Singapore, Beijing, Shanghai, Hong Kong, Bangkok, London and even Johannesburg ... getting me to partake of the best of *sake, shochu, sashimi,* sushi and the likes of my favourite *tempura, yakitori* and *omurice* to delicacies, specialities and everyday foods ... *kaiseki, teishoku, wagashi, okonomiyaki, oden, motsu nabe, shabu shabu, sukiyaki, don buri, onigiri,* even the famed *fugu* and many, many more. Each one of them was not only a gracious host, but opened up with stories, perspectives, anecdotes, interpretations and learnings that I have used in various contexts in *Japan Made Easy*.

My most valuable content for this book has come from my various interactions with Japanese colleagues of mine who worked with me in India during my Dentsu days. Seichiro Hayata, Kenji Nogami, Takemi Furuta, Atsushi Kurokawa, Takashi Koyanagi, Hiroshi Omata, Norimichi Uno, Akifumi Miyahara, Hideto Azuki, Koichi Fukumoto ... each of them deserves a big bow of gratitude from me for enriching me through their knowledge and understanding of their home country and its unique culture, and for taking the time to share with me all they knew.

Krishan Chopra was the editor of my first book, *The Dum Dum Bullet,* way back in 2004. He was again my editor for *Konjo – The Fighting Spirit*, in 2014. *Japan Made Easy* would not be a reality today without his guidance and support as the publisher and boss-editor. My thanks also to Ananya Borgohain and Bonita Shimray from HarperCollins who have shaped the content and the aesthetics of the book through constructive suggestions and valuable inputs.

A big thank you to Jaideep Mahajan (JD) from Rediffusion for the wonderful cover of this book, and for the oh-so-Japanese illustration hand-done by him.

This book would just not have seen the light of day without Manali Sawant, my assistant, who tirelessly inputted all the copy; and without my nephew Mukul Rai Bahadur, who formatted, cleansed and re-arranged the book at least half-a-dozen times, given my limited IT skills. A big thank you to Manali and Mukul.

Finally, as I write the final pages of this labour of love of the last eight years, I miss my mother and my mother-in-law, both of whom left us within a month of each other, earlier this year. My mother, Kailash, has always been my inspiration. And the one who willed me to greater heights, greater conquests. Mama would have been delighted to see this book in print. My mother-in-law, Shanta, was my biggest fan. My writings always made her very proud of me. This book would have been a joy for her.

Last, this book is more Tanya's and Carol's than mine.

Tanya is my 24*7 encyclopedia for events, happenings, experiences, words, meanings, names and nuances. She remembers everything for me, especially all the hard stuff that I want to conveniently forget! More importantly, Tanya is my ignition, keeping me charged and committed when quitting the writing was so much easier. This book needed me not to stray the course. Morning after morning, Tanya would ensure that I was at my writing desk ... and getting me to do that wasn't easy!

Carol was responsible for a lot of the research and content validation needed for this book. She was more focused than I; she was more industrious too. She slaved through many of the voluminous reference books I brought home over the years from Japan, highlighting relevant paragraphs and making copious notes I could speed-refer to. Carol has been the backbone of this odyssey.

Thanks, hugs and kisses to both my brave ladies, Tanya and Carol.

In closing, a tearful thank you to Jambo, our pug, and my constant companion through the writing of this book. He curled up every single day at my feet, participating in my progress through his cuddly presence. Alas! Jambo left us before the book could hit the stands. But his loving contribution will always be much remembered.

ABOUT THE AUTHOR

Dr Sandeep Goyal, 56, is a nipponophile, having visited Japan more than a hundred times over the past twenty-five years. He actually considers it to be his *karmabhoomi*.

He was born in Amritsar, did his schooling at St John's Chandigarh, got his Honours in English Literature (with a gold medal) from Punjab University and then did his MBA from FMS, Delhi. He also holds a doctorate in Business Management from FMS. Sandeep is an alumnus of the Harvard Business School (HBS), having attended the prestigious three-year OPM programme.

Goyal started his career in advertising with Hindustan Thompson Associates (HTA), now known as Wunderman Thompson. He then worked at Trikaya Grey and Mudra before going on to become the president of Rediffusion - DY&R at the age of thirty-five. Post that, he became Group CEO of Zee Telefilms, India's only listed media company at that time. In

2003, he partnered with Tokyo-based Dentsu Inc., the world's single largest advertising agency, in joint ventures for India and the Middle East.

Over the years, Goyal has handled many of Japan's top global brands including Toyota, Honda, Suzuki, Nissan, Yamaha, Hino, Bridgestone, Canon, Sony, Panasonic, Toshiba, Hitachi, Fujifilm, Casio, Seiko, Citizen, Nissin, Ajinomoto, ANA, JAL, Shiseido, Kao, Unicharm, JETRO, and more. So, he has a deep appreciation and understanding of Japanese business.

Goyal has been on the global advisory bodies of the National Academy of Television Arts and Sciences (NATAS), New York and MIP TV (US). Goyal has been on the governing bodies of the Advertising Agencies Association of India (AAAI), the Indian Broadcasting Foundation (IBF), the Media Research Users Council (MRUC), the Advertising Standards Council of India (ASCI) and other industry bodies.

He was the first Indian juror on the Global Emmy Awards, and has graced the juries of many other prestigious awards in India and globally. He also writes signature columns for *Business India*, *Business Standard*, *The New Indian Express*, blogs for Campaign, an agony aunt column for exchange4media and guest columns for *ET BrandEquity*, *Mint*, *FirstPost* and others.

He has authored three books before this: *The Dum Dum Bullet*, *Konjo - The Fighting Spirit*, and *BlogBuster*.

Goyal is also an ardent collector of ceramics and studio pottery, including some priceless Kakeimon and Imari pieces from Arita.

He is married to Tanya, also an MBA. They have one daughter, Carol, who is a lawyer by training. The Goyals live in Mumbai.

www.ingramcontent.com/pod-product-compliance
Ingram Content Group UK Ltd.
Pitfield, Milton Keynes, MK11 3LW, UK
UKHW040759130726
13719UKWH00011B/123